# THE

# TRUTH

# ABOUT

# 911

Fiction….?


All the people that would not have received a PARDON has died. It is now time for the American people to know the truth. No matter if they have the strength to handle it or not.

I do not ask for any forgiveness, for I surely do not deserve any. I only pray the memories of the nightmares that I have endured for what we did to our country, will along with my soul burn up in the flames of HELL!

## Chapter One

It was a real dark, dark, dark, night. Quiet and eerie, where there was no motion of wind and only total silence in the air. Suddenly, a lightning bolt flashes through the sky. The whole world seems to light up as the Thunder roared for all to hear.

Jake Peterson jumped up in bed startled, he tried to settle himself down as, his heart was rapidly beating like it was coming out of his chest. Jake had been in a deep sleep, but instead of being upset by the loud crackling sound, he welcomes it with joy. It had awakened him from a nightmare that he was having.

Jake quickly grabbed his neck and sprung from his bed, rapidly heading for the bathroom, he tripped over his shoes that laid at the bottom of the bed. He hastily got up and ran into the bathroom still clenching at his neck.

He could hear his heart pounding as, he grasped his neck, he thought he felt warm blood running down his arms.

He hastily flipped on the light and stared at his mirror as his eyes filled with fear, he clutched at his neck. He roughly rubbed his hands across his neck and saw no blood, then he started to realize that it all was just a dream. A nightmare that seems just too real.

He then felt a warmness like blood down by his genitals. He quickly looked down only to discover that he had pissed on himself. The dream had scared him so bad that he urinated some into his briefs. "Oh shit!", Jake said as he stared down at the wet yellow stain.

Jake tried to collect himself, trying to slow down his breath, as he smiled then laughed at himself in the mirror as he was so relieved that it was only a dream and that he was still alive. As the nightmare started to slowly fade from his memory, he was relieved that he was now starting to just remember part of it.

It seemed so real, nothing like any dream that he has ever had in his life. As, it started to fade from his memory, he could only now remember certain parts of it.

He remembers walking down a dark street alone, he heard a noise and realize that there was someone following him. He could hear footsteps speeding up, as they approached, he wondered who could it was? He began to turn to see who was bearing down on him. Unfortunately, before he could see who it was, he felt something going across his throat.

He quickly reached for his neck, he felt his own hot blood oozing out of his throat, pouring over his hands and rushing down the front of his chest.

He found himself gasping for breath, then he felt the cold wind come rushing into the back of the inside of his throat. The cold wind came in through the opening gash, that he felt his fingers go in, as he held his neck.

He started to lose conscience, he felt his body become totally limp then he fell toward the concrete sidewalk. He noticed the dirty blowing trash that littered the street, he managed to turn his body when going down.

In an attempt, to see who had done this to him. He fell onto his back feeling his last breath rushing from his body, he looked up to see who had cut open his throat.

BOOM! All he could remember now was the loud sound of thunder that woke him from his squeamish nightmare. It was over, he didn't care who it was, because now he was so relieved that it was a dream, it was all just an awful nightmare.

He giggled at himself in the mirror, as he talked to himself out loud. "Shit, oh, boy, that shit seemed so real, oh hell, what the hell did I eat last night?"

He laughed at himself as he took one last look at his neck to insure himself that it was just a dream and that it never happened.

All he could remember vividly now was the loud sound of thunder, that had rescued him from his worst nightmare. He smiled one last time for himself, breathing a sigh of relief, as he walked slowly out of the bathroom and headed back toward his bed. Rubbing his neck for it all seemed so real!

Still shaking a bit and half awoke, he went stumbling across the kitchen. He reached up to his cabinet over the

4

refrigerator and opened it revealing a half full bottle of Johnnie Walker.

He smiled, he reached for it pulling it down from the cabinet and quickly unscrewed the top. He looked over to where there were some china cups, but then decided to lean back his head, he held the bottle to his mouth and took a big gulp and swallowed, to clear his head.

Aaaaah, oh yeah, he said. He screwed back on the top and placed the bottle back into the cabinet, saying that hit the spot all right. He started to feel more reassured of himself, as he rubbed the top of his head.

He headed out of the kitchen as he continued to gather himself and asking himself why he dreamed such a crazy nightmare. He still was a bit unsteady due to the dream feeling so real. The dream kept fading away from his memory, his heart was still racing faster than usual, he felt a chill over his body. He had no idea of the gruesome nightmare that he was about to soon face, except this time he would be wide awake!

RRRRRRINNNG!! His alarm clock went off startling him, he hollered…" Damn!" Then he quickly ran toward the bedroom, tripping over his shoes that he laid in the middle of the floor, as he made it over to the alarm clock and forcefully shut it off. He then said... "Work", as he quickly went from the bedroom into his bathroom and cut on the shower.

He pulled down his briefs, he took a quick glance at his vanity mirror, just to double check once again on his neck, as he lifted his head checking for a cut, and laughed at himself for being so stupid.

5

He finished taking off his briefs, he then stepped into the shower adjusting the spigot to take a nice warm shower. He started to suds himself, his hands moving the soap across his neck, he could not help but to look down at the soap to see there was any blood on it. He laughed at himself again, as he said... "Man, what a nightmare?"

He leaned his head back, the warm water came down upon his face, he washed his hair and rinsed it with the escalating water flowing from the spigot. The water spraying across his face sending a warm feeling but, a false sense of security that everything was going to be all right.

Jake finished his shower and quickly dried off walking back into his bedroom where he could get dressed for work. He put on his suit as he pulled out some matching socks to go with his suit. After, putting the last sock on, he discovered that a hole was in it showing his pinky toe. He said to himself, "Huh... nobody will see it", as he started putting on his shoes.

After, putting on his shoes, he started to tie the first shoe, when the shoe-string broke after, he pulled it to tie the knot. "Damn, he said, I can't believe this." He quickly kicked off his shoes and went over to the closet to get another pair to wear. Which of course, did not match his suit.

He finally got fully dressed, grabbed his briefcase and his keys and headed toward the front door. As soon as he had opened the door the phone rang, he quickly wondered if he should answer it? As, he decided to close the door and race over to pick up the phone. It was one of his co-workers asking about him coming to work today? He said yes, I am on my way now, what is it?  The co-worker said it can wait, I just wanted to make sure that you are coming in today.  The co-worker then hung up.

Jake then thought to himself, what the heck could that be about.  He then thought it not my birthday, they could not be arranging a surprise party.  I don't think he called about us getting a raise, maybe someone is leaving, they setting a go-away luncheon?

He hung up the phone and opened the door and went out, quickly reaching in his pocket for the keys to lock the door, as he turned and started heading for his car.

Walking down the walk toward his car, he saw his neighbor up ahead of him.  It was one of his neighbor who owed him some money, for an old car that he sold the guy's nephew and it was over a week late getting the final payment. After spotting him, he hollered to him as the  neighbors quickly jumped into his car hollering that he was late, he would get with him this evening when he gets home.

Frustrated, Jake just balled up his fist and said..., "never again."  He continued walking down the walk disgusted at not getting all his money up front before releasing the car to the guy's nephew.  That what happens, you try to be nice, I guess one day I will learn, he says to himself.

He then hurried toward his car trying his best not to let it upset him.  He approached his car, Jake hollered, "Give me a break!"  As he stared at his car he could see that it had a rear flat tire on the driver's side.

He thought to himself, I think this is going to be one of those days, I should have stayed in bed.  Jake did not know how right he was, things for him would end up being a lot better for him had he just stayed home.

He thought to himself, I am going to be late for work now, I better give them a call. He reached for his phone pulling it out he then realized that he did not need to call them. They have already called him earlier, he told them he was coming in. He put the phone back into his pocket and walked over to his car opening the door and tossing his briefcase in.

He then started rolling up his sleeves and opened his trunk and started getting his spare tire out. That is, when he realized that the new car that he bought did not come with a spare tire or a donut tire.

It came with a little pump-up inflation kit instead of a spare tire. After taking fifteen minutes to figure out how it worked, he was finally able to get his tire pumped up and now was finally ready to go to work.

Jake pulls out his cell phone to see what time it was and thought to himself... I guess I won't have time for breakfast with the guys today. He jumps into his car and headed out for work, as he thought he better grab something to eat before getting to work.

He pulls into a local mom and pop shop restaurant and get a coffee and a bagel. He then jumps back into his car and headed toward work. Thinking about why his co-worker called him this morning, what that was all about?

He pulls up to a red light and decides to reach for his coffee to get a quick sip then suddenly Bang! The car behinds him bumps into his car causing him to waste coffee on his white shirt. "What the hell", he shouts, he looks behind him and see a young man with a puzzled look on his face in the car behind him.      He      says,      "Damn fool", as he put his coffee cup into the cup holder in his car, as he jumps out to confront the driver.

As, he approached the driver in the car he remembers seeing the car at the restaurant.  The driver in the car is sitting there with an empty cup of coffee and a breakfast platter all over his lap.  Jake hollers, "Kid what is wrong with you?" "Don't you know you are not supposed to eat and drive?"

He berated the young man then looks at his car and was relieved that there was no damage.  All the accident cause was a little coffee being spilled on him and a coffee and a breakfast platter spilt on the young guy.

Jake was already late for work, he felt there would no need to wait for a police officer, there were no damage to his car.  He hollers at the young driver, "I hope this will be a lesson to you don't drink and drive."  He then stormed back to his car, spitting in his hands, he tried to wipe the coffee off his shirt.

After driving for a while, he finally arrived at his place of employment.  A firm by the name of Mundy Investments.  As soon as he pulled up into the lot, he saw people standing alongside the building, they were scattered throughout the parking lot.  He pulls up to one of his co-workers and ask, "Is the building on fire?"

"Worst", the angry co-worker shouted to him, "we have been Fired!"  "Fired, what", Jake said, "we are fired?"  "Yes", said the co- worker, "we, all of us, it seems that Mr. Bates been running a Ponzi scam with this

9

firm." As his co-worker hastily walks away, Jake can see more black SUVs coming up into the parking lots and agents dressed in suits with guns strapped underneath their jackets or on their hip going into the building.

His first thought was to gun the engine and get the hell out of there. Then he thought, wait a minute they are not arresting any of my co-workers, they probably only after Mr. Bates. He thought, I better go up and clear my desk of stuff, before everything is confiscated.

Jake pulled into a parking space and hurried inside as he saw more people rushing out cursing and swearing that they have just lost their livelihood. That is, when it finally struck him, I don't have a job now? This has been the worst day of my life? Unfortunately for him, the day was not over yet?

Jake went into the building and jumped on the elevator and he rode it up to his floor, he could not help, but think, what in the hell am I going to do now? I just bought a new car, now I don't have a job, how am I to pay my rent? Ding, the elevator reached his floor then the doors open.

Before, he could get out, a woman with a box of stuff jumped on the elevator crying. He quickly moved around her and got out. He saw two other guys coming down the hallway cursing. "I told you", one said to the other, "I knew these mother%$$ were crooks, I told you, I told you, didn't I?" Jake quickly passed them and headed toward his office.

Jake walked toward his office, he passed the CEO's office. He heard voices coming from a door that was open and there were some agents in there talking with his boss. He stood to the side of the door trying to listen to find out what was going on. His boss then turned his head toward the door and saw Jake.

Jake, there you are, come here, come here. Jake startled he thought to himself, what come here, what the hell you want from me, this fool better not act like I knew anything about this? His boss, Mr. Bates, hollered again, "Jake, Jake, come here!" Jake hesitantly stepped into the office as he saw standing on the other side of his boss, two uniformed police officers who quickly turned around and started looking at him. Then his boss said, there he is officer, this is Jake Peterson."

Jake was in total shock as everyone turned and stared at him. "What, what, no, not me, I didn't do anything, I didn't know", Jake said. He then looked at his boss and shouted., "You son of a bit%$!" "I knew nothing about this, I did not know you were running a scam." "You no good bastard trying to throw me under the bus, I know nothing, nothing, he did, it was all him." The next instance, Jake lunged toward his boss, yelling I am going to kill you!"

One of the officer grabbed Jake, when he approached Mr. Bates, saying to hold it to Mr. Peterson, we need to talk with you. Jake screamed, "I didn't do it, I didn't do nothing." "It was him, it was him not me, I knew nothing about this." "I was not involved in this scam at all, he is lying, that son of a bit%$, I didn't know he was stealing the investor's money?"

The police officer then threw Jake upon the boss's desk as both officer wrestled with him as one of them put handcuffs on him. Jake was still screaming "I didn't do it!" Mr. Bates looked pitifully at him and said "Jake if I knew you needed money this badly, you know I would have loaned it to you". Jake screamed, "He is lying it was all him, officers you have got to believe me, I would never take investor's money." One of the officer then said, "I don't know about any investor's money, we are here for you robbing the liquor store!"

"The what", Jake shouted, "robbing what? The officer said, "The Wimberly Liquor store on Fifth and West street." "Witnesses saw your car, there were no tags on the car, a good Samaritan followed it and reported where you abandoned it." "We traced the serial number, it led us to you."

"What, what my car is outside, I did not rob a liquor store", said Jake, "what are you talking about?" The other officer said, "Read him his rights. Jake's boss, Mr. Bates, shouted I will get you a lawyer, Jake why did you do it, you know we keep plenty of liquor here, why didn't you just steal some from here?"

"What, what", Jake asked as he was still not understanding what they were talking about. "A liquor store, I never robbed a liquor store", screamed Jake!

One of the officer then said, "Sir, do you own a red 2001 Toyota Celica?" "Yeah", said Jake, "oh no, no, I mean I use to own one, I sold it to my neighbor's nephew." "It is not my car anymore, that was over a week ago." "I have not seen the car, honestly, you can ask my neighbor?"

The other officer then asked, "Mr. Peterson, who did you sell this car to, do you have a bill of sale?" "A bill of sale", said Jake, "no, no, it was an old car I just sold it for cash he hasn't fully paid me yet?" "Well Mr. Peterson", said the officer, "you do not fit the witness's description, what was the name of the guy?

"His name", said Jake, "I don't know, I know his Uncle, he is my neighbor, I sold it through him." "Mr. Peterson", said the officer, "since the car is only registered to you according to the motor vehicle administration, you are going to have to come down to the station with us, until we can get that cleared up."

"No, no, his uncle can tell you", said Jake, "he is one of my neighbors." "Do you have his number", asked the officer, "is he home right now? ""No", said Jake, "and he was leaving when I left, but I did not do it, his nephew has my car." The officer said, "I believe you, you don't know the full name of the person whom you sold the car?" "You can't produce a bill of sale showing that you sold the car." "I am sorry, we are going to have to take you in, until we can figure this out."

"What?", said Jake, "you said you believed me, I didn't do it." "I know sir", said the officer, we have a warrant for you." "We cannot release you until we have straightened this out." The police officer took Jake by the arm and said, "Sir, this way please."

"Wait Jake pleaded, "I just lost my job, I am going to lose my new car and apartment and now I am going to jail, oh God!" Jake, took a big deep breath and knew it was not worth fighting, he had to go with them until, they could locate the nephew.

The officer then started escorting Jake down the hallway and into the elevators, Jake feeling depressed and hopeless just held his head down. Once, reaching the ground floor they started walking out to the parking lot as Jake looked up and noticed that everybody was looking at him. He walked with his hands behind him bound by police handcuffs as everyone turned and stared.

Then someone in the crowd hollered, "Look, it's Peterson, he was in on it!" "Get that no- good thieving bastard", an old lady hollered! The next thing Jake knew was that stuff was flying in the air toward him and the police officers. "Kill him, kill him", the angry mob shouted as the police quickly rushed him to their cruiser not only for his safety but theirs as well.

As, the police quickly raced out of the parking lot, he could hear people screaming and cursing talking about Vengeance is the Lord's, we are going to find you, you can't hide. Kill him, kill him, I never did like that beady eyed son of a bit%$! As the crowd kept hurling stuff at the police cruiser as, they quickly sped away.

After, they finally got away from the mob, one officer called into the station that they had picked up Jake Peterson. The dispatcher then relayed back to them that the warrant had been lifted, the perpetrator had been captured, he turned himself in and confessed to everything. "Well, Mr. Peterson, it looks like you didn't do it after all", said one of the officers.

"Yeah", said the other officer, "but from now on always make sure you know who you are selling your stuff to and always get a bill of sale, in case you need to verify it."

"Now to get you back to your building, if you want to go back there?"

Jake hesitated, then said, "My car is back there." The officer turned around and drove back to the building after taking the handcuffs off Jake. They told Jake to squat down. They did not want him to be seen, as they approached the parking lot. Once, they got to his car they all quickly jumped out as the police stood nearby in case the crowd noticed him.

Jake quickly started up the car and drove out of the parking lot as people noticed that it was him and started throwing things again. After travelling for several blocks, he came upon a red light that he had to stop for.

Taking several deep breaths of relief, he rolled down his windows. He shook his head, as he tried to get himself together. Trying, to put the pieces together to figure out what had just happened? Saying to himself, it couldn't get any worse. He was wrong.

Just then, suddenly, a car comes flying down the street. It slams on the brakes stopping just beside him. Jake turned with fright, as he looked thinking that it was one of his crazy co-workers that had followed him. As, he stared at the car, he saw a guy that he did not notice as an uncontrollable fart came out. Jake, hope it was only a fart and nothing else.

Then suddenly, the guy looked over at him, then toss a briefcase into his car and speed off through the red light. Terrorist... was the first thing that shot through his mind, as his bladder then gave him a jolt!

"I can't believe this, haven't I had enough today?" As Jake sit there waiting to blow up, he then saw a black car and a black SUV racing down toward him. They both zoom through the red light trying to catch up to the car that just threw the briefcase into his car.

Jake was so distraught, that he just sits there, the light changed green and Jake just kept sitting. He then started coming to his senses, as he asked himself, why would a terrorist blow me up or my car. Terrorist usually blows up building and stuff where they can kill several people.

"What in the hell is going on now", he thought to himself as he looked down at the briefcase. Then someone drove up behind him and started beeping the horn!

Jake threw up his hands saying, "All right, all right", as he drove through the green light. Jake drove down the street looking over at the briefcase that the man threw into his car. Now, that he had convinced himself that the briefcase was not a bomb. He then started to wonder what could possibly be in it?

Should he take it to the police and tell them what happened? Who was the guy that tossed it into his car, who were the two cars chasing him? The real question that he thought about was, could it be full of money, probably all cash non-traceable money.

Maybe, money that had been stolen from the firm that someone did not want to be found with. Could finally his awful day start to get better. Finally, after all the bad luck that he had been having today, he finally found the silver lining in the dark cloud?

Maybe today will not turn out to be such of a bad day after all. This, he thought to himself, could make up for my job I lost. I wonder what is in that briefcase, he said smiling to himself hoping that it turns out to be what he was thinking?

He finally drives home, he picks up the briefcase and walks to his door, as he kept thinking of what is inside of it. He enters his place and go over to the coffee table in the living room and place the briefcase down.

Next, he heads for the kitchen, opens the refrigerator and grab a cold one and twist off the top. He goes back to the living room, as he falls on the couch and take a big swig and then burps, "Buuurrrpps!"

Oh boy, he giggles to himself, I needed that after all I have been through today. He suddenly looks down and stick his hand between his legs as he lifts himself up. Then sniff his fingers, just double checking that everything is all right down there.

AAAaaaaaaaaaa, oh yeah, he says, smiling again, as he looks over toward the coffee table. He wanted to open the briefcase, hardly able to wait, but at the same time enjoyed the curiosity of not knowing what was inside. He knew, once that he opened it the wonderful curiosity of not knowing what it possessed would no longer be there. It sounds strange, but in a funny way, he did not want to lose that strange feeling of not knowing, what lies inside. Where sometimes a person's imagination can be more pleasurable and enjoyable, than the true reality of what exist.

Like a child at Christmas, he sits there for a while. For, is the joy really the opening of the gift sometimes, not finding what you wanted, or that feeling before opening it, hoping that it is that pony that you have always wished for.

Jake sits there smiling at the briefcase, hoping that it would turn out to be that pony. Then reality crept in, if it is money could it had been stolen and traceable by the police, or could it be drug money? Money belonging to a crook who may of saw him throw it into my car?

Then he assured himself, no, no if that was the case the guys in the other vehicles would had stopped at my car and retrieved it. Nobody knows I have it.

He reached out and picked up the briefcase, but still the thrill feeling of not knowing what was in it made him put it down. He wanted to be able to fantasize a little bit more about it.

He was like a gambler, holding onto his horse race-track ticket or lottery ticket enjoying the feeling of the chance of winning before the race ends, or before the winning numbers are called.

He decided to wait, just wait a little bit longer, excited about finding money in the briefcase, but at the same time fearing that all he may find as some rumble papers and an old man's stale sandwich that his wife prepared for his lunch.

Only time would tell, but for now, he decided that it was worth waiting a little longer, just in case, he does just end up with just turkey on rye.

As, he sits there on the couch thinking about all that happened today, and what the briefcase will bring him, once he opens it. He decided he wasn't quite ready yet to guess what was behind door number three, as he thought about the old game shows.

The excitement that everyone feels before the door opens and one discovered blissful happiness or sadly discover they should have kept the money in the box.

Jake decided to turn on the tv set for some entertainment before getting up enough nerve to open the briefcase. He started watching a talk show as, he started to unwind from all the hectic of the day, when another thought came to his mind.

What if the guy in the car that threw the briefcase in my car got a good look at me and track me down to get back his money?

No, no they were moving too fast, they wouldn't recognize me again if they saw me. They were panicking, all they know is the guy might have thrown the briefcase out of the car onto the street somewhere.

There is no one way that they could possibly remember my face. They were moving too fast to even get a glance of my car, they did not even notice me. I am sure that I had my head turned opposite of their view when they went flying by.

Wait a minute, what about my car? They did drive up on me from behind, did they see my license plates? They could be tracking me down right now, finding out where I live?

It's a good thing I did not open the briefcase, maybe I should wait a couple of days, and then if I don't hear from anybody, then open it. Yeah, yeah maybe I should wait.

Jake then started flicking through channels on his tv when he came across the news. On the screen of the tv was the picture of the guy that threw the briefcase into his car.

He choked on his drink as he quickly used the remote volume button to turn up the sound on the tv set. The news person reports that the guy was found shot to death in his car. Not only that but, the guy was a United States Congressman on the Intelligence Commission.

After, hearing that Jake quickly turned his head and looked over at the briefcase and gasped! Now he was even more intrigued than ever and knew he had to open the briefcase.

He knew a lot about Congressmen and how they accepted large amount of money under the table by Lobbyists and now he was sure that he had hit the Jackpot.

Maybe some lobbyists had paid for him to get some vote passed in Congress and it was not successful, so they wanted their money back. Could have been one of those lobbyist bidding on million dollars contract in the Middle East, a payoff or something like that.

Now Jake was really convinced that there was money in the briefcase. Now he was more intrigued than ever as he questioned himself about just how much money he would find in inside the briefcase.

Jake picked up the suitcase looking at the leather design on it as he flipped it around looking all over it, and then sniffing it Sniffing it in between the opening and saying, huh, doesn't smell like no stale sandwich to me? He then laid it down on the table and decided that now was the right time to open it    He laid it back down on the coffee table in front of him and put his thumbs upon the latches and pressed. The latch was locked, he laughed to himself, oh you are locked, well this is not going to stop the big bad wolf from getting in, heh heh heh.

DING DONG! Aaah, Jake said as he knocked the briefcase off onto the table onto the floor. He was startled and started asking himself, who could that be? Could that be someone who knows about the briefcase, and they have tracked me down? Ding Dong, the bell rang again!

Jake tried to steady himself, as he slowly got up off the couch and crept slowly toward the door as the doorbell rang out again, Ding Dong, causing Jake to jump. After reaching the door he slowly peeked out of his peep hole in the door, when he heard. Jake, Jake, are you home. He looked out through the peephole he could see a familiar face. It was his neighbor, the Uncle to the nephew that he sold his car to.

"Shit!" said Jake, as he quickly unlocked the door cursing as he flung the door open. As soon as the door opened a handful of money popped up in his face. "Hey Jake", the Uncle said, "I got your money, I got your money." The Uncle saw the look on Jake's face and said, "Hey buddy I got the money, all of the money that Jason owes you for the car." "I got the money for you," the Uncle said, as he hesitates and then asked, "Buddy is anything wrong?"

"Wrong, wrong", said Jake, "what could be wrong?" "It just another average day, every day I get carted off to jail and body slammed on my boss's desk like a slab of bacon"!

"What, what are you talking about", said the Uncle, "what happened to you? Who did that?" "What", Jake said, "who did that,

21

the cops did that and all because of your nephew!"

"My nephew, what,", said the Uncle, "my nephew called the cops on you?" "What", said Jake, "no, the cops got me because they thought I was him." "What", said the Uncle?

"No, I mean", said Jake, "your nephew, your crazy nephew, did you know he was a criminal?" "He used my car to rob a place, and the cops came looking for me."

"Oh no, God no", what" said the Uncle, "no I didn't know the cops contacted you." "I just found out about him robbing a liquor store and his mother made him turn himself in." The Uncle asked again, "The cops came after you?" "Yes', said Jake, "he never registered the car and was driving it and they traced the car to me!"

"Oh Lord, I am so sorry Jake", said the Uncle, "I am so sorry", I would have never told you to sell him that car if I knew he was that type of boy."

"Yeah, yeah", said Jake, "but it too late now, but I can tell you one thing." "I have learned one thing from all of this, the next time I get a new car, I am going to trade in the old one no matter how little they give me for it."

"Oh Jake", said the Uncle, "I am so sorry, so sorry". "Here, here take the money that he owes you", said the Uncle, "I am so sorry". Jake grabs the money and shakes his head as he closes the door.

He walks back over to the couch and put the money on the coffee table as he sits back down on the couch. He tried to erase the episode that just happened outside his door as he started to focus back on more important matters, what was inside the briefcase?

He tried to calm himself and control his breathing, as he said to himself, no sense of me getting all riled up over something that has already happened, I know better next time.

He then said to himself, "ow where was I, oh yes, the briefcase, we must open the briefcase." He went into the kitchen drawer where he kept some tools and took out his screwdriver, holding it up saying, this should do it.

He went back into the living room filled with excitement, as he sits down on the couch placing the briefcase at the edge of the table then held the screw drive to his lips and kissed it saying, my little gold pick, heh. He then stuck the screwdriver under the left latch and started prying the latch until it popped opened. He smiled as he said, one down one to go.

He started on the right latch. Pop, it opened as Jake smiled, as he started to raise the lid. Jake felt that as soon as he lifted the lid of the briefcase it was going to change his life. Unfortunately, for him, not the way that he was thinking?

Chapter Two

Slowly the top of the briefcase opens as Jake with a hopeful grin on his face raised the lid to reveal the contents. He saw what was in the suitcase, the only word that he could only muster out of his mouth was," …What?"

The content of the briefcase that now was exposed, was not the million dollars or even diamonds or jewels, that he had suspected and hoped for. For all that his eyes saw was some papers, just old documents and a DVD.

"What in the hell is this", Jake said to himself, as he started to realize that his dreams of being rich had just vanished before his eyes. He then reached into the briefcase bringing out one of the vanilla folders, as he stared at it, as he felt his joyfulness leave his body. This was not what he had expected to be in the briefcase.

He slowly opened the vanilla folders to look at the papers inside of it. The first page that he came across read...To Whom It May Concern.

It went on to say... If you are reading this, I am probably dead and let me tell you that my last wish was that these papers did not end up in the wrong hands.

My last prayer was that finally this vital information will be shared among all citizens of this country. That we, as a people, finally put an end to this madness that we have been allowing to fester in our country's government for far too long.

My only regrets that I have are due, not to my safety and life, but for the welfare of many innocent others. I have reluctantly allowed for this conspiracy of our government to continue far too long than it should have. Not having the sense to realize that a government is not transparent to its own people, it assures that corruption, injustice, and a move away from democracy is totally inevitable.

As a true patriot of this country, unfortunately due to greed and fear, I cannot say that I have always been patriotic. Let alone truthful or honest to the American people. However, in some small way, I hope these pages that you are about to read will not absolve me from my wrongness, but simply in a small way allow me to beg you for forgiveness.

I know that I cannot right the wrongs of this country that I and many others, along with me, and even before me have done to a country that once was America the Beautiful.

It has now become a country of hatred, greed, imperialism, injustice, and the opposite of a true democracy.

Hopefully, I am dead, for I would rather die finally doing something good for my country instead of serving life in jail for all the wrongs that I have allowed to be done to my country. I regret what I have allowed this country to go through. Hopefully, now these pages will bring about a new revolution that will make America great again.

I am just as guilty, as those that I speak of, I too like many in Congress. I did not have the will power, the strength, too much greed for the money that we could make. Simply, there were others who just did not give a damn for this country. I confess that I am guilty of all imaginable and much worst.

Where should I start? In my long career in politics, I can still remember, when I was first sworn in. I remember the words I spoke, as I stood there before Congress. I do solemnly swear or affirm that I will support and defend the Constitution of the United States against all enemies foreign or domestic; that I will bear true faith and allegiance to the same.

As, I look back now, it seems that I forgot the domestic part. For to bear true faith and allegiance you must remember that it does not only apply to foreign enemies, but to your fellow Americans as well. Our forefathers knew that our biggest enemy that could harm us the most, is not a foreign one but an enemy from within our borders, within our Congress, within ourselves.

I just like you, have been brought up all my life believing that this country of ours is the greatest country in the world. Maybe when we were young and growing up, it may have appeared that way back then. I ask you as time went on, has it not changed? When you place your right hand upon your heart and look at that flag, does it blow in the wind as glorious as it once did?

I believed in honesty, fairness, equality, truth, justice, and what we consider the American way. However, while in this Congress, I have gone against everything that I once believed in. God, have mercy on my soul. No, no, change that, for I deserve whatever punishment is bestowed upon me. Be it on earth or in Hell!

I will never forget the first time that I was elected to the House of Congress. I was young then and a rebel, who had plans to make this country not only great, but one that every single citizen of America could be proud of. During that time of segregation, we had not achieved it for many black people, even today not every American is treated equal.

I was so young, so vigor, so liberated, and was determined to make this country a country for all men and women to be proud of. Little did I know back then, that like many like me, instead of changing Congress for the good of America. I too eventually let Congress change my views, as I became part of the so-called good old boy club.

We are all taught at birth it seems, during our early childhood during puberty, that America is a great place. We have it memorized in the back of our minds so much that even our own eyes cannot tell us anything different. In our schools of learning, we are taught to believe what we are told by our gov't that provides the books to teach us to become good citizens.

In our Civic and History classes, we repeat great quotes from the past. Famous quotes from our forefathers and revolutionaries who said such things as, my only regret is that I have only one life to give for my country.

We are taught, as soon as we can read, to be proud of our Independence. That through the revolution that we fought and died for during the American War. A fight for Freedom, instead of being a subject of a British Empire, we created a country where all individuals were to be declared that all men are created equal. Yet, even then we did not see all Americans equal, for we did not include women, let alone black people that we enslaved.

We formed a government of the people for the people, and most of all, by the people. A gov't where the people have the power, where the people choose who they want to represent them, not some royal rich family choosing what rights they choose for them. Not the rich royal minority, but the common man and woman who are the majority would be the ones that control this country's government. That was then, this is now.

We are no longer a gov't of the people, let alone by the people. Instead of us having a gov't that looks out for the welfare of the common man and woman, we now have political leaders that only look out for themselves. Just like the Midas Rule, he who has the most gold rules.

We have gone from a people's democracy to a full blown outright Capitalistic Oligarchy. Where once upon a time, we were a humble country that sought peace and the worship of God, now we have become a country that seeks out war and only worship the mighty dollar.

That is why our money is stamped with In God We Trust, our trust is not placed on the Lord in Heaven. We have allowed our gov't to place it on their mighty dollar. That is why we must stop our gov't from replacing our Trust of God that reside only in our heart.

For we must have it removed from their sinful monetary notes. For it is said that the love of money is the root of all evil. I ask you, why do we allow them to place God's good name on that which causes so much greed and hate among us.

Oh, when I was first elected to office, I was so proud that I could not help from smiling, I felt so good that I just couldn't stop. I was sworn in to become a servant of the people, not a ruler of the people. You see, that is how it was meant to be.

However, anyone that believes in one person one vote such as what we use to have in this country, but not anymore. For the people allowed its gov't to create Superdelegates who share more voting power than almost a third of the American voters in each party. We have no one person one vote, we have no democracy, let alone a country of the people, for the people, or by the people.

I first was elected into Congress, I had no idea that there would come a time where America would sit idly by. While their country leaders are chosen by a few hundred so called unpledged delegates that can outweigh the vote of millions. Have we forgotten who we are or where we come from?

I have often asked myself, how did we go from a country of the people, to a country of the rich and royal. That which we fought to get rid of, now we have them ruling us again.

Is the apathy for our country that strong, or have we simply given up on everything we once believed in. We have allowed our country to become a country ruled by the rich, that which we fought to get away from.

I once believed in such things as justice, liberty, and freedom. Yet, what I see now is only a farce to hide the real greed, hatred, and imperialism that we have allowed to take over our democracy.

My fellow Americans, where did we go wrong? How did we not see this coming and when it came, why did we do nothing about it?

It took the biggest tragedy attack ever known to this country, to take place on our civilian shores since the American Revolution. I excuse Pearl Harbor because it was an attack on our military, not a direct attack on civilians. Such a thing that most modern-day citizens thought could never happen.

Being the most powerful country in the world, who in their right mind would be stupid enough to attack us? The United States of America, not only did we believe no one would ever attack us. Even the rest of the world knew no one could be that dumb to attack a powerful country like ours.

Not only, every citizen of the United States, but every person across the world will never forget that day. September 11, 2001, the day that will never be forgotten and we can only pray not be repeated.

None of us will ever forget watching the breaking news that a plane somehow flew into one of the twin towers. That early Tuesday morning will always be remembered in the minds of all Americans. A tower that is over 1300 feet high and an airplane with open clear sky could not see it and simply fly around it.

The first thing came to our mind is how is this possible? How could the pilot crash into such a tall building? Did the plane malfunction and the pilot had no control or was he drunk? We all sit in disbelief that such a terrible air traffic disaster like that could happen here in the United States.

For us, that all it was, that all it could had been. We helplessly watch our television sets, as we ask ourselves how could something like this happen?

It was like the Hindenburg's air disaster, it was simply unbelievable that something that tragic could happen. We watched in horror as we saw the huge cloud of black smoke pillaring from the building.

Knowing, that not only the terrible lives of the passengers in the plane were all destroyed, but also many of workers in the building. Who lives were also destroyed or in danger as the smoke from the building kept rising into the sky. The most unimaginable air disaster one could possibly see on tv, until a few minutes later.

When suddenly, a second plane goes crashing into the Twin Towers! At first, we thought the news were showing a repeat of the first plane. As we gather our thoughts and common sense and just then we realized that this was no air crash mishap. Not one, but two planes have flown into the Twin Towers!

Like the Pearl Harbor attack, we knew it was a day that will always be remembered. Except hearing about it later, this time we saw it happen live right before our eyes on our television sets. We soon received reports that other planes were in the air that may be flying on a suicide mission. Or as you like, a hari-kari attack on other cities around our country.

The President was taken out of school (a school that he was visiting) and rushed to safety as we heard about a plane heading toward Washington DC, then minutes later finding out that American Flight 77 slammed into the Pentagon.

While another plane, United Flight 93, was hi-jacked. As brave American citizens fought to take back the plane from the hi-jackers. They were able to prevent it from carrying out it drastic horrendous mission as they forced the plane to crash in a field in Pennsylvania.

Immediately alarms were set off, as government buildings went on alert and offices all over including schools were shut down. As we realize that this was no accident, that our country was under attack. NORAD took to the sky and all commercial aviation came to a complete halt as all planes were ordered to land as soon as possible, until they could figure out what the hell was going on!

The whole country was in shock and total disbelief as phones ranged all over America. People calling their friends and love ones to advise them what was happening. To find out if they were safe? Our first concern at that time was defense, to protect our citizen lives and try to stop from any more lives being taken.

As things calmed down a bit, later that night our President came on to explain what in the world was going on. However, before the world saw the President speak, I and others intelligence contacted him and informed him that we were investigating to see who was behind this horrendous attack.

Before, we could go any further in the conversation the Vice President insisted that there are no questions about it, that it was the work of Saddam Hussein. He the Vice President, not the President insisted that we attack him immediately!

We, the intelligence staff, all strongly disagreed with him, as we argued back and forth. Then the President finally spoke up saying that the American people are waiting for their leader to make a statement on the air. I need to know what I am to tell them?

The Vice President interrupted, you tell them the truth, that Saddam did this and we are going to get him, Damn it! Then he quietly whispered under his breath, something that your daddy should have did.

The President did not appreciate what he said, and I especially did not appreciate it either. Since I was the main person who had his father put an end to the Desert Storm War. After I started arguing with the Vice President, the Secretary of Defense got involved. Everyone knew that I could not stand the Vice President and he felt the same way about me.

I was so pissed off, I was ready to go for his eyes. Everyone saw what was about to happen and security was called to clear the room. The President was upset and said, we have enough shit going on right now, we don't need this!

Before, I left I insisted to the President that until we find out for sure who was behind this. He must tell the American people that his heart is with them and the people we lost. Promise them that whoever did this will face our American Wrath and pay dearly. Tell them that you must ask for their patience for now, but you promise them that those responsible will be dealt with.

As I left the room or more like pushed out of the room. I was sure that when the President spoke to the people that he was going to say something like what I had just told him. Boy, was I wrong.

As a serving member of the active advance team of the Intelligence Committee, I along with others knew it was up to us to find out who was behind this. None of us could believe the nonsense that we had just heard from the Vice-President. As I said to the others, I got to figure out a way for the President to get rid of that bastard. When it comes to starting a war, he is ten times worse than Hitler.

The bastard looks like that Sgt. Hans along with his sidekick, the Secretary of Defense who looks like that Colonel Klink on Hogan's Heroes, doesn't he?

The guys laughed as they said come on we got work to do. The White House, or I should say, the Vice President was all gung-ho to blame this attack on Saddam, which did not make any sense. Without any proof, no facts, he was convinced that it was Saddam for some unknown reason?

However, we were not going to jump to that conclusion without hard facts. Since we knew just about everything there was to know about Hussein. For him to be behind this, we knew it just did not make any plausible sense.

Knowing now, that we have been attacked by some outside forces. That our peaceful daily lives had been interrupted, and that they would never be the same again, from this day forward. Our sorrow quickly changed into revenge as we ask ourselves, who are the people? What person in their right mind would attack a powerful country like ours? Who could possibly have such nerve, such audacity to attack us on our own shores.

Our embassies have been attacked over in other countries, but how is it possible that some outsider could come in and attack us from within?

As we started getting information from across the world from our different international intelligence. We became more convinced that Saddam had nothing to do with this. Yet, as we worked diligently to find out who was behind this tragic attack, we were soon interrupted! As John Blane came rushing through the door and turned the overhead screen on and turned to the local news.

I was wondering why he was wasting our time hearing what the President was going to say. When we were busy trying to find out who did that, so the President would be able to inform the American people later. Yet, as I heard the President speak, I then realized why he turned the channel on. John said, I just heard about this over the news wire, look what is coming out of the White House press!

As the President spoke and told the American people along with the rest of the world that we had been attacked by terrorists. However, he did not mention at that time anything about who it was.

He told the country to be strong and pray and that we would bring the culprits to justice. However, it did not take long before the White House staff later released to the press that it appears to be a man by the name of Saddam Hussein.

As this information flooded the media, our country was no longer a country of pain, sorrow, and sympathy. It was now a country of complete total outrage and looking for revenge!

I myself, and the rest of the people in the intelligence field was in total disbelief. The White House had over stepped us and reported something that we felt 99% sure was just a plain lie. I could not believe what I was hearing being broadcasted to the American people.

I just then received a call from the General, who ask me if what he was seeing on the news was true. I told him… Hell No!

The General and I were close, and we were both dear friends of the President's father. I think that if anyone disliked the Vice President more than me, it was him. He had seen war on the battlefields not just new reports on a television set. He knew the horrors of war both physically and mentally.

He knows what it feels like to tell a mother that her only son will not be coming home. To stand in front of a big strong strapping young man and then look down and see that both of his legs are gone.

The General knew that all wars are hell and you only fight them when you have no alternative. You never start a war until you are one hundred percent certain. Not only that, but also that you can end it and ending it as quickly as possible.

Unlike those who never set foot on a battlefield, or held a friend talking to him as he dies in your arms. When it comes to war, we must not make any quick judgements or a mistake. Because mistakes destroy lives, not for the foolish politicians who make these mistakes, but for our children who are the ones that must fight these wars.

As I sat there in our meeting room listening to the News media telling the people that Saddam had attacked our country and we were getting ready to bomb the hell out of him once again to get our revenge. I knew that the first time we attacked him, we did not have all the facts, and once again we were about to do the same thing again.

I sit there asking myself, a stupid question, why did the White House allow the release of these statements? Why did they not wait until we had verified it? Knowing full well, why the President did it, just like many other things that he had done. Listening once again to my favorite Vice President?

It spread like wildfire across every television station across America and the world. I could imagine the look on Saddam and all the Iraqi people when they received the news. Saddam and many other world leaders, especially those in the Middle East made urgent calls to the White House, but no phones were being answered. The White House had made it decision and it was going with it no matter what.

I am sure that many like myself, felt if this country was ever attacked it would be by none other than some country that has great power, like Russia or China. Now the world is being told that the Chihuahua has attacked the mighty Great Dane. It goes against every rule of nature and every bit of common sense.

Suddenly, Senator McFee stood up and said, Gentlemen, I did not get the memo what in the Hell is going on? The same thought that was running through all our minds. As I ask myself, why in the world, would Saddam do this, why now, especially now? When we are on the verge of re-opening relationship with Iraq due to the high price of oil. It just did not make any sense?

During a meeting on the following day, when asked about the allegation that Saddam Hussein had anything to do with this attack. I quickly spoke out and said, at this time, we do not know who is responsible for this, but I can say to you 100% without any doubt, that it was not Saddam Hussein.

When asked who I thought it was, if it was not Saddam. I told them at this time it could be anyone else. We know that the hijackers were citizens of Saudi Arabia on the plane, but at this time I cannot verify 100% who was behind this attack. We are gathering international information from all over the world, trying to see if someone heard or seen anything.

At this time, I will not release to you any rumors or unsubstantial facts that have not been verified. I can only state fully with 100 percent accuracy that Saddam and any party officiated with Iraq had nothing to do with this attack.

When I was pressed at how I could be so confident that Saddam was not behind this unless I had a pretty good reason of who was behind this. I repeated, I do not have any confirm 100% approved data on that subject and I will not release any information until we do.

However, let me make it perfectly clear that we will leave no stone unturned. We are looking everywhere including here in the United States! Let me assure you that we will find out who or whom so ever may have had any involvement in this attack. The meeting then came to an end without any more questions after I said that.

Ever since the Desert Storm War, we have had full intelligence watching Iraq and Mr. Hussein not only on the ground and air, but even in space. We have used satellites to monitor his country and we probably know more about what goes on in this country than our own. Therefore, we were convinced that Saddam did not have anything to do with any attack.

Still for some time, the White House did not report our findings as the media kept telling the American people that it was Saddam and his terrorists in Iraq.

Many Senators, including myself, was calling the White House constantly to have him notify the news media. Instead of that happening my favorite Vice President and others associated with the White House went on talk shows and anything they could get on. Saying that Saddam not only did it, but that he was possibly having contact with Al-Qaeda.

Finally, it was not until other countries, started proving through their intelligence that Saddam had nothing to do with is, is when the White House finally stopped accusing Saddam. All our calls to the White House was not being answered or returned and the President seem like that he was still in hiding.

As our investigation continued, it started to become more clearer and clearer that no outside force could have accomplish this without inside help. We had evidence from people who knew the terrorists that were on one plane who were not Iraq, but all were Saudi Arabians. With the knowledge that Saddam was not behind this and knowing that due to the rising cost of oil that pressure was on the government to lift the Iraq Oil Sanctions that was put in place after the Kuwait invasion.

The first thing to come to mind is who would benefit from this, other than the oil sheik of Saudi Arabia? Not only did all the people who was traceable were all from Saudi Arabia. Most of all, if the United States ended the sanction on Iraq, that would have had a drastic effect on the demand for Saudi oil. We started tracing through our intelligence in Saudi Arabia to find out more about the Saudi Arabian terrorist who were on the planes.

What the White House had did, by accusing Iraq before we had a chance to investigate brought a sickness to my stomach. It reminded me how we rush to invade Iraq when it was reported that Iraq had invaded Kuwait. Saddam just woke up one day and decided to attack Kuwait? It did not make any sense then and how quickly once again the White House had rush into declaring that Iraq had attacked this country.

I started to recall how Kuwait told us how they were being attacked and how instead of us having the sense to ask why? The White House just assumed that it was not provoked. I remember when we finally found out the truth and how quickly the President ended the Desert Storm Operation immediately.

Desert Storm, the truth that most Americans, even today, do not know the truth about. Before I continued with the bamboozle of 911. I think that first, to get the American people to believe that which they do not want to believe. We must go back to

Kuwait and the battle that is referred to as Desert Storm.

For 911, was not the first time and I am sure will not be the last time, that our government lied to the American people. The Iraq invasion into Kuwait that took place back in 1990 was a time that I will never forget. The White House received an alert that Iraq had invaded Kuwait and was in the process of taking over some of their oil fields. It was soon reported that precious oil was being burned, oh and some lives being destroyed.

Let me tell you at this time, I remember all the reports that the White House received about Rwanda genocide that was started also in 1990. Over a million people were murdered or as some would say genocide. I bring this up to make it clear to you that we did not take part in Kuwait due to any people. No, as always in most cases due to protection of their precious resources which in this case was oil.

It was during the Iraq attack into the land of Kuwait, that unlike how we stood by while millions of people were murdered in Rwanda and did nothing, that the President quickly move into action. Of course, this did not come about until after he received calls from many rich oil associates. The President immediately sent our troops into Kuwait to rescue the oil.

When our intelligence reported to us that Kuwait had been invaded, I was at first stunned that Saddam would do such a thing. With all the oil that he has, why would he want or have any need to expand? The first thing we needed to do is to contact our people and see how this came about. I am a

41

strong believer that nothing comes about overnight, it takes time and a reason for any war or battle to take place.

The average person may think that any oil country could be attacked due to their abundance of precious oil. Yet, because of that oil, they are protected. Because if any country attacked them to obtain that oil, those countries, like the United States, who receive and benefit from that oil would not hesitate to attack any invading country that tries to take that oil. Therefore, Iraq that has more oil than it needs, why would it be so stupid to invade another oil country knowing that the United States would have no choice but to get involved.

Many Americans may have a false belief that America is a peace seeking country, that will quickly come to the aid of any small country when humanity is in question. They may see America is being concerned for the welfare of others and may even view America as seen as a humanitarian in the eyes of the world.

However, whenever a country like the United States which is large and powerful as it is. Knowing the horrors that were taken place during Rwanda, Sierra Leone, and many other small countries, seeing this type of inhumanity going on for years but sit back and does nothing. Let me assure you that we are not humanitarians as much as we are greedy Capitalist.

Yet, when precious materials such as oil as in danger and the rich capitalist gets on the phone, it does not take long for aid to come rushing in.

It is reported that during that time in Africa, over a million lives were destroyed as the rest of the world stood by. People were raped, sodomized, tortured, decapitated legs and arms chopped off.

As the terror of a Genghis Khan swept through their humble villages and no one saw any godly need to assist. When their cries of pain shot across the world, we like others had a deaf ear. However, when precious oil is tampered with that is another story.

Unlike turning away like we did with countries in Africa who had no oil. It did not take long for our capitalistic gov't to hurriedly move to put a stop to the mere thought that precious oil was being wasted. The main reason being when you help a country that only facing human genocide than helping a country that can benefit you with oil. To any capitalist country like ours it is an easy question.

Some of you may say, what about the holocaust, did we not help the Jews? Hitler had taken over countries and murdering Jews for a long time before we got involved. We did not get involved in any humanitarian way to protect the Jews, but to only protect ourselves from the probability that we may be next. Once he had built up a big enough army from all the countries that he was taking over, we knew sooner or later he would come for us.

May I remind you again that our country is never going to get into a war, unless we know that it will benefit us either in the short term or the long term. Usually all wars that we find ourselves in are due to money, not humanity. People may speak of believed that we are country of Democracy. Yet, look closer even at our government to see that we are a country controlled and lead by Capitalism not Democracy.

When Intelligence oversea inform us of the invasion of Kuwait and especially that it was Iraqi army that had invaded, it did not make any sense. What was Saddam smoking? Was the man on drugs or not taking his meds? Why in the world would Iraq invade Kuwait, when he knows there is no way we would sit back and let that happen. If he had invaded maybe Rwanda, ok, but a rich oil country, now he knows that a no-no.

What came across to us at first was that Saddam Hussein just woke up one morning and decided instead of having a V8, he would have an invasion into Kuwait. However, before we had a chance to find out what was going on. The White House after receiving its big Capitalist donors' calls had place the military on alert and we were on our way to Kuwait.

It did not take long before we were contacted by the Iraqi government, that explained the reason for the invasion. As they said that they were invaded by Kuwait, not the other way around. All while we were trying to solve this the invasion by the United States forces continue as we started Desert Storm Operation.

There were many in Congress who wanted to invade Iraq and they felt that their long-lost dream had come true. Now we have a reason to go after Saddam and get him out of office. I believe that is why it took so long for the White House to finally accept our conclusion from our investigation.

When the President abruptly put an end to the war and especially stop the movement into Iraq, need I say that there were plenty of Congressman and rich Capitalist associated with the oil who were pissed off as hell!

The President knew if he stopped this war, that a lot of his financial supporters were going to be more than just upset. He knew that what he was going to do was going to guarantee that he would not be re-elected. Yet, he still did the right and Godly thing and finally put a halt to the Desert Operation before we took down Saddam.

The Oil companies, the rich businesses, and Wall Street had the end of Iraq right in their grips and then it was snatched away from them by the President. They wanted to denationalize and privatize the Iraqi oil trade and they knew by getting rid of Saddam, they could put in his place a puppet that would allow this. Needlessly to say, I think if they thought they could get away with assassinating him, they would have.

What our intelligence found out about the Kuwait invasion and that which we were able to verify, was that Saddam was right. It was the stupid Kuwait military that attacked them first. It turns out that Iraq did not invade to take over Kuwait's oil fields to sell for profit, but only went over to set fire to some of their oil fields. Which of course, did not make any sense either, at first.

Once again, it involved the mighty dollar, the love of the root of all evil. What took place between the two countries remind me of my old school days. The school teacher is at the board writing down stuff for her students to learn. Talking to them and then turning around to clarifying what she is saying by writing it out on the chalkboard.

While the teacher's back is turned, the little boy, let us call him Kuwait, decided to have a little fun and throw a spitball at the big boy in the classroom, who we will call Iraq. Of course, right as Iraq send the spitball back hitting Kuwait in the face, this is when the teacher turns around. Without hearing any excuses, she immediately kicks Iraq out of class and send him to the principal office.

Of course, it is not until later after class that the teacher goes down to the Principal's office to check on Iraq and then Iraq finally gets a chance to tell his side of the story.

The boy Iraq has already been embarrassed and sent into the Principal office and now it is up to the teacher to decide what punishment he should receive Since, it was not him who initially cause the disruption in her class, but the other boy who did. who not receive any punishment, hopefully the teacher will not force the boy to stay in the office.

The right thing to do is to confront the other boy and let it be known that horse playing is not allowed in class. At least, bring the punishment against the Iraqi boy to an end immediately after finding out the truth. This is what the President did once he got the complete story, he did the right thing, he put an end to a problem that should have not arose from this dumb situation in the first place.

This is like what happened with Iraq and Kuwait. Of, course instead of spitballs, money was involved. Kuwait interested in making money they decided to make financial loans to Iraq. It was at a high-interest rate, but since Iraq had no plans of ever paying them back, they did not mind that.

So, after a while, just like when you may have loaned your friend, or should I say so- called friend some money that you expect back in two weeks. After two months, you start getting concerned if your friend or even relative is going to pay you back.

Similar things happened with Kuwait, eventually they saw that Iraq had no intentions of ever paying back that loan. Now, some us may just say, well a lesson learned. However, most of us, especially when it is a large amount of money, would more likely say, damn it, I am going to get my money back.

The latter is what Kuwait said. They were not about to lose all that money, so instead of chalking it up as a lesson learned, it was time to teach Iraq a lesson, a lesson called Bi#$# better have my money!

The next step that Kuwait took, after threatening and repeating asking that came to no avail, felt they had no other choice than to teach him a lesson so that he knows that they mean business. In other words, Kuwait felt that it was time to stop playing around with Iraq and it was time to kick some ass!

Kuwait took it small army and invaded Iraq and just went in far enough to place some troops around a small oil field in Iraq. Then told Iraq that they would release it once they got their money.

However, Iraq did not find that funny and Suddam must have asked himself, are these fools crazy. They are going to come into my country, take over an oil field and then tell me, that I better pay, if I want it back? It did not take long for Iraq to send an army out to take back the oil fields.

This is when Kuwait realized just how stupid this move was, as they quickly deserted the post and ran back home. However, it was not over yet, Iraq felt to teach them a lesson so that he would not have to go through this again. He decided to now invade their country and take over their oil fields. Not to keep or steal their oil but set a few fires to let them know not to ever try that shit again.

This is when Kuwait decided to holler bloody murder, that they were being attacked, not explaining why, but what seems to the United States, attacked for no just cause.

Once we finally found out why they were invaded, the President felt that lives were more important than a few lost dollars from a rich man's pocket and decided to put an end to the war.

With all the money that these Middle Eastern billionaires have, he made the decision to end the war immediately before any more lives were wasted on either side. Which I was proud of to hear and knew unlike many others in politics, lives meant more to this President than money. It was time to bring our troops home, and the oil people were madder than Hell!

It had been a long time since I was proud of a President, or any member of Congress in a long time, for that matter. It may me think about when I stood with him during his inauguration. Which I tell you was the coldest day, it was freezing, and it was so cold it must have been snowing in hell. Now, I did not mind catching that awful cold on that day, when he declared an end to this war, it was all worth it.

Even after finding out the truth, it was the President's decision that we need not publicize the reason for the quick end to the war. Many Americans wondered why we stopped the war so quickly, especially when it was going so well, and we could have easily taken out Saddam. However, we knew that would be like punishing the schoolboy for something that someone else did.

Also, we knew to keep the Middle East stable, we could not risk taking out a strong head figure like Saddam. It would surely create chaos and even if we put a puppet in, it would surely cause problems with all the radical groups who would probably rise and create a much bigger war than the one that we were ending.

The President remembered the disaster that we went through in the Middle East when we try that before with Iran. Oh, yes, I remember, our American backed Shah, Mr. Mohammad Reza Shah Pahlavi, the Shah of Iran. What a mistake that turned out to be.

I was so glad that I was not about to see history repeat itself. Like the old saying, sometimes it is better to try to work with the bad one you know because the new one you don't know may be much worse.

I remember how we assisted him in the takeover with a coup that was based upon not only the U.S but also some allies. I guess I don't need to tell you why, of course oil as usual. The country of Iran had its oil nationalized at the time under the Prime Minister Mohammad Mossadegh. Which of course, we did not have control of the Iran oil the way the U.S. oil companies would have it.

They would much prefer it to be more privatized. To be able to bring in the foreign oil firms to make money. We knew that under Mossadegh that was not going to happen, so we made a deal with the Shah that we would take him out with a coup and he in return would allow us control of the oil distribution.

Unfortunately, later not to his modernization and western thought, but because of greed and capitalistic behavior, eventually he lost the support of the working class and religious groups. Putting thousands of outspoken citizens in jail who spoke out about his wrong doings. Eventually the people had enough, and a revolutionary take over started to take place.

As the political unrest increased and we discovered that we did not have as much control as we thought with his thinking. As we tried to veer him in another direction to soothe the people, but he felt that what he was doing was right. As we watched the Iran revolution turn away from Western views and become replaced with a national Republic.

The Grand Ayatollah Khomeini came to power after the revolution. Which of course was not what the United States government wanted, but this is what happens when you put the wrong puppet in. Just like marriage, you might love them the best at first, but through time they can change causing them to become worse than what you expected.

Just like another, old Noriega, Mr. Manuel Noriega, our dictator over in Panama. I knew my friend well, I worked closely with him on U.S. intelligence. He was a valuable resource to the CIA and helped us a great deal with counterinsurgency forces throughout Central and South America. However, after the publicity of his rampage drug dealing, we knew that we had to ask him to slow it down and make it more private.

Of course, with all the money that he was making from illegal means, he decided to ignore our warnings. Eventually we had no choice but to go and take him out of office and put him in jail where he belongs. He like so many others were a victim of greed, power and stupidity. He had us close on his side if he behaved and did what we told him. Yet, like so many, they outgrow their pants and think they are bigger than what they are. Let just say he out stayed his welcome.

We asked him to at least direct a great deal of his drugs that was coming into the United States away for a while. Just temporarily due to the American media making it their lead story every night. Due to all the things that he helped us with in intelligence in the lower America. Instead of killing him we decided that jail would be better. Knowing that once things cooled off, there would be a likely chance that he would be transferred back to Panama or some other country that he would like.

As I think of the major coup and the countless mini coup that I was involved in. As I also think about all the many coup that our government has been involved in throughout history. There is only one guy that I will always remember. I will never forget Mr. Untouchable, Sir Teflon, the great Moby Dick, the one that got away. The one who got away time and time and time again. The man must have been a damn saint or Lucifer himself.

We tried so many times, so many times, so many different plans to take him down, but nothing ever worked. We tried killing him, taking him out with an overthrow, everything we could come up with, but somehow, he always escaped. He was my Moby Dick, the one that got away. Fidel Castro is the one man, I will never forget.

Let this old man stop reminiscing, let me get back to 911 and why we knew it was not Saddam. The reason why I brought up the Desert Storm Operation, because that was when the Intelligence team started making Saddam it's top priority. After Desert Storm, we scrutinized Iraq like a germ under a microscope

After Desert Storm, we had heavy surveillance on him and he knew it and that is why I knew there was no way that he had anything to do with 911.

At that time, I knew Saddam and Iraq were not responsible, but unfortunately at that time I did not know who was responsible, or proof at that time. As I ponder on who was behind that, I knew one thing, that whenever some crime happens, 99% of the time is has something to do with money. So now I just needed to follow the trail and it would lead me to the pot of gold.

After Desert Storm, there were many people, not only those in the rich establishment, but even the average citizen who were upset with us not taking out Iraq. So, to keep face and make things more acceptable, we decided to place sanctions against Iraq.

This would cripple it, but it would not hurt Saddam, but only the citizens of Iraq. Also, it would benefit Saudi Arabia to lessen any competition in the oil distribution to the U.S. and other countries, now that Iraq was sanctioned.

The sanctions stayed in place from 1990 until 2001, when due to the high cost of gas, and the complaints from the American people. The Congress was considering lifting the sanctions due to the outrageous price of oil. Many in Congress felt that Saddam and especially the innocent people of Iraq had been punished enough.

The price of gas has jumped drastically, and unlike in 1970s fake gas shortage by the scam of OPEC to raise the prices, the American people knew the cause was simply greed and nothing else.

However, back in 1970 we did not have a country that had been sitting on its oil for over ten years and was itching to sell oil to us at any reasonable price. This time the American people had a solution to the high price of gas, as they screamed oil is oil, just lift the Iraq sanctions.

There was a great deal of pressure put on Congress to lift the sanctions, which would have been a wonderful thing for the American people. However, a terrible thing for the Arabs and especially the rich in this country not only those in the oil sectors, but many sectors. For many rich American investors had invested into Saudi Arabia. Not only in their oil fields but building the country up.

With the investors of the oil section many had signed long term leases to purchase oil at a set price. A slightly variable price based on the economic effects adjustments, etc., other words greed. This would insure not only that oil would be available, but also more U.S. import control in the future.

However, the oil was just one sectors, the oil of course used a great deal of wealth which was provided through the American banks. However, also provided by American Banks were loans that were given to Saudi Arabia for what some may call western modernization. However, most of us would more likely call it Glitz and Glamour.

Saudi Arabia was building like crazy and importing all these American contractors over and paying whatever price they ask for. Why not, if they charged too much just give it to them and make up for it when you raise the price of your oil that you know they are going to buy. It was a win-win situation for the big banks, big business and corporations, where everybody was getting rich and to pay for it all, just raise the price of gas on the American people.

They were building buildings everywhere, building house everywhere, even out in the sea, they had hotels everywhere. Building skyscrapers all over and without any idea of ever using them, it was just art decor. Billions and billions of dollars of art-deco, but why not, when it was not going to cost you anything, you just pay it from all the money you get from the U.S. who is buying your oil.

They even had people skiing in the desert. They were thinking up everything they could do and knew that the well of wealth would never run dry. Everyone drink and be merry, and a lot of United States companies came and helped themselves being paid outrageous prices.

The banks wrote out loans to anyone for any price. You could build a small dog house and get a million-dollar loan for it. Cause they knew that as long as the oil flowed they were going to get paid back.

Everything was wonderful, when money got a little low, hey just raise the prices, which they did. Unfortunately, this time the American instead of just accepting the rising prices of oil, like they did in the past, many ask, what about all that oil that is sitting over there in Iraq doing nothing? Saddam has been quiet, not bothering anyone, we think it may be time for him to get off with good behavior and his time out has been served.

Now, suddenly, the shit was getting ready to hit the fan. As lobbyist flooded the Congress explaining that they could not lift the sanctions. Not only because of all the money that the Saudi owed American companies, not only because of all the money that the banks had loaned them, but also all the money that the banks had them deposit into the U.S. banks. Where they deposited because of the high interest rate that the banks were giving them that was much higher than the American people were getting. However, don't think it was just the banks. Our own government had borrowed ridiculous high interest loans with Saudi Arabia.

Now, suddenly, Congress realized that lifting the sanctions against Iraq, would not only have drastic effect on the Saudis, but also will have a great effect on the wealthy and big banks in this country. Let alone what would happen if the Saudis called in all the loans made to our government and said pay up or else.

So, the Congress tried to go to the Saudis and explain the dilemma that they were in.   They suggested that Saudi Arabia lower the price of oil to U.S.

The Saudis said no problem, I will lower the price of oil and you will cancel all the money that I owe the United States for all this building that you have been doing over here, overcharging me for.   I will let you break the news to your American companies.

The Congress knew that they were not going to go back and tell them the Saudis has been excused from paying billions of dollars to their companies and bank loans.   Now Congress found itself between a rock and a hard place.   The arguing continued in Congress, as the American people got more outraged.   Saddam would eagerly ready to give to the American people, all the oil that they want and at any reasonable price that they want.

It was like Saddam was going to hit the lottery and Iraqi oil would be flowing to the United States again, but who then would buy Saudi's overpriced oil?   As the arguing continued in the Congress, it seems that Saudi Arabia was going to get the short end of the stick.

In private meeting, they just laid it out on the table explaining how much money not only from the banks, but from corporations, and investors.   Including many Congress people who invested into the boom in Saudi Arabia.

As this nonsense continued for days, as people kept complaining back and forth all the pros and cons. I remember a lady Senator by the name of Jane Snow, who stood up to speak before the Senate and said...

"I do not have enough fingers or toes, to count how many times I have seen this body of law, a law that is supposed to be for the people." "Yet, go against the people, against the mass majority, all for the sake of the small minority rich". "It is a shame, that you have the nerve to call yourselves, a representative of the great people of this country, when they are always placed in the back seat".

"Time and time again, I have seen the welfare of the millions be ignored, just for the monetary benefit of the minority rich." "Not this time, not this time." "If the Saudi will not give us a temporary drop in price of oil during this economic crisis in our country, we have no choice, but to lift the sanctions and let the chips fall where they may".

As more people stood up to speak, anyone could see as time went on more and more people started to lean toward lifting the sanctions. It had been ten years, there are some who have committed murder in this country and due to copping a plea or good behavior have done less than that amount of time.

Especially, since we knew that Kuwait attacked his country first. I think everyone knew sooner or later the vote had to come and it would be for the lifting of the sanctions.

I will never forget when a young newcomer stood up at the podium, who was pissed off that a decision had not been made. To him and most of everyone else, they knew the only decision, was that, if Saudi did not lower their prices, we would have to lift

Iran's sanctions. He stood there laughing as some giggle with him and said..., "My dear Congressmen, believe me, we must lift the sanctions." "It would take an act of war, an attack from Iraq, for the American people not to demand these sanctions be lifted." "We have no choice, we have wasted too much time already, let us do our job and lift these sanctions."

He received a standing ovation from most of the attendance. Many who were doing everything they could to stop it, knew then that it was going to happen, and nothing was going to change it…. we thought.

It was less than a week later; a plane flew into the Twin Towers! Therefore, I knew, as many, when we heard that nonsense that Saddam had something to do with this horrible slaughter. There was no way possible, it went against any common sense. Saddam and Iraq had so much to gain.

If we had been attacked right after the end of Desert Storm when the sanctions were put in place, that I could believe. However, to attack right before we lifted the sanctions, after not attacking all these years.

On top of that our intelligence knew that he did not have the capability to pull something like this off. No one has that type of capability … at least not without a whole lot of inside help.

No country in this world would do something like this, they would know, we the United States would bring down the Wrath of God upon them. As more intelligent information came in, we realize that more and more, it looked like an inside job.

Like a person reporting a robbery in their house when we see where the robber came in. After looking at the broken window and then realize that broken glass was on the outside of the house, not the inside.

Any fool could see that Saddam would not gain anything from this, but, who would? Who were about to lose so much if the sanctions were lifted? Once again, the path of all evil lies where the money leads you.

As I spoke earlier, there were many in Congress who was upset over us ending the Desert Storm Operation. The same people who thought they were going to make a killing, a monetary killing, during Desert Storm.

Many saw Desert Storm as a gold mine that would last for at least ten years and the money from gov't contracts from weapons, food, construction, etc., were going to make them filthy rich.

They saw the invasion into Kuwait by Iraq as their piggy bank. Now the game was on again and even after proving without a shadow of a doubt that Saddam had nothing to do with 911, we should have known that they were not about to give up that easily.

As I think back of the days when Saddam was a close confidential ally of our government. How well he allowed us to use him to go after his neighbor Iran. We supported him with billions and billions of dollars, planes, weapons, guns as well as chemicals. In hope that he would be successful at taking out Iran.

We convinced him that with our help that he could take over Iran and we would together rebuild it. You see, Saddam liked our western views and ideas. With his help, we were going to spread our ideology into Iran and eventually throughout the Middle East.

If it had not been for us promising him our full backing, he would have never tried to overtake Iran. We promised that we would make Iraq the prominent dominant Persian Gulf state. We were successful in getting a revolution coup offense to take place in Iran. We decided that with the disturbance we had created in Iran, it would only take an outside attack from Iraq to be successful at taking Iran down.

I personally felt that we overestimated the Iraqi army or underestimated the Iran army, whichever one chooses. I think we should have trained them more to make sure that they were willing to go and fight relentlessly.

However, soon after the war started, they were not used to death and I think they lost the will to fight. Over a million people were killed, most of them civilians, and once again what seemed like a good idea, did not turn out that way.

Even with the use of sulfur mustard and chemical weapons that we provided them, we should have known that they needed to be trained. As they face the wrong direction of the wind and probably killed more of their own than they did the Iranians.

However, hopefully, we learned from our mistakes. For other countries knowing that the West was backing Iraq, it only made more Muslims support Iran. Later we would find out just how much that war backfired in our face.

Many, many years later, the United States spoke out about Saddam using chemical weapons against his own people, but he would have never had the chemical weapons to use, if we did not provide them. More importantly, they were dissidents from what our western ideology was, and we approved 100%.

We encouraged him to use them so lives of his own soldiers would not be taken. Just like we used the Atomic Bomb that saved a lot of our own soldier lives during World War II.

Of course, like always oil played a part. We knew we only had a certain amount of time to get this accomplished before it put a huge burden on the Middle East oil trade. Finally, for us our time clock ran out and the pressure from the oil business came flooding into the White House and we had Iraq start a retreat from the country of Iran.

Saddam may not have been able to topple Iran, like we had hoped, but because of him, we were able to get a stronger foothold over into the Middle East. It is funny how quickly loyal friendship can change sometime as quickly as overnight. One would be surprised at how easy it is for one to be a close friend one day and the next day become one worst enemy.

It is amazing how some people are, how relationships can vanish once they no longer need you to do their dirty work for them. Yes, I knew Saddam had nothing at all to do with 911. However, when it comes to the American people, they can be so easily hypnotized by what they see on a television screen.

I don't think the news media has any idea the huge effect that they have on the average citizen. Most of them will believe anything that the media tells them without even using common sense, to understand that anyone can make a mistake.

Even worse, I guess that they believe anything coming out of the White House. Yet, our country had just been attacked, our citizens were still stunned in disbelief, and I guess at a time like that you are vulnerable to believe anything.

Even after the news was falsely telling the American people that Iraq was behind this. Still the news reported that on the hijacked plane that only Saudi Arabians were discovered on that flight. Yet, still everyone listened to the White House and went along with it, instead of saying Saudis were on the plane, could it be that they may have had something to do with this?

The White House was determining to go after Saddam and Iraq and the American like sheep just blindly followed along. We, in the top-secret intelligence knew that we could not let the farce continue. Finally, only through the help of other international intelligence, the White House saw that this was not about to work.

Yet, they continue with it hoping it they said it enough times, that would make it true. When they finally realized that this plan was about to explode in their face, they rush to find another scapegoat. For they knew that once the world realize that it was not Saddam and Iraq, then the question would be, then who? Who had the nerve to attack this country and when are we going to strike revenge against them?

They had to act quickly, there is an old saying that goes, if you do something wrong, and if you can't think of a person to blame it on, then just say…the Devil did it. America's devil at that time was an old chap by the name of Osama Bin Laden.

Of course, the people were so upset that they were ready to go after anybody, so who better for them to go after then the Devil himself. The no-good scoundrel who just like the real Devil was kicked out of grace with the Lord. The same way that Osama was kicked out of grace with the United States.

The old Devil Osama Bin Laden, who American at least our gov't and the White House once praised as the chosen one. A hero among angels when he successfully defeated Russia and kicked them out of Afghanistan. Well, at least that how we thought of him during the war before it finally ended, and Russia had to withdraw after their defeat. A defeat, let me say that was possible from a great deal of help from us.

Back during the end of the 1970's, a lot of shit went on during the 70s, Russia invaded Afghanistan. The United States backed the Afghan people 100% and assisted Osama in every way we could. Even if he did not want our help but knew that he would not be successful against Russia without it.

We gave them weapons, military training, money, money, money and more money to prevent Russia from taking over Afghanistan. No, we did not do it for the Afghan people, oh no and Osama knew that.

We did it for the same reason we got into the Vietnam war, we did not want Communism influencing the Middle East. We knew if Afghanistan was taken over, it would probably not be long before Communism would spread across the Middle East.

Osama, was no fool, he knew this, he knew that we were not supporting him because we felt it was a humanitarian thing to do. The only reason why we were supporting him was because we were not going to just stand by and watch. As, influence and ideology start taking place without doing everything we could to stop it.

We did not only provide weapons and training, but of course our own special forces to make sure that Osama would stop the Russian invasion. Osama reluctantly accepted our help, and I think the President should had known that he owed us no favors after the war. Yet, the President thought differently and for some reason thought that after helping Osama, that he would allow us to set up at least one military base. We try to use fear, what if Russia decides to attack again.

If you have one of our military bases over here, we can guarantee that you will never have to worry about Russia ever attacking you in the future. Our President thought for sure that after Russia left that we would be able to move in. However, I remember Colonel Eastwood after going over to meet with Osama and something that he told me when he got back. He said, I have finally seen the Devil in the flesh and I think the President is making a huge mistake if he thinks that man will ever accept us.

I can tell you during our meeting, that he hates us more than he hates the Soviets, and there will be no relationships with us after this war. I honestly believe that the men that we have trained and the guns that we have provided may one day be facing us.

He tried to get the President to listen, but there was no way he could convince the President. The President just knew that after helping Osama in getting Russia out and Osama into power, just like so many dictators that we had help, Osama would side with us just like all the others.

The war lasted longer than I had expected. Over ten years including the coup that most people do not know about. The war ended with nearly two million deaths and countless refugees fleeing the area. Back before the war started or before Bin Ladin went into Afghanistan.

We assisted Nur Muhammad Taraki, who was head of the Democratic Party of Afghanistan and after a quickly bloody coup, he was in power and was replacing the Muslim way of life with radical modernization reforms.

Just like all dictators, the power went to his head. Due to paranoia, he started killing not only his political opposition and prisoners, but also many who were friends and allies. Eventually, this lead to a revolution and Russia did not hesitate to move in when they saw the door was open. What we had plan on doing with Taraki, now Russia was doing it against Taraki, because of his terror that he was inflicting upon the people.

So finally, when Russia was convinced that the continuation of the war would not be beneficial and was not a cake walk like they had expected. Russia finally decided to start withdrawing their troops from Afghanistan.

Before a year was up finally there were no more Russian troops in the country. As Osama and the Afghans celebrated, we did not wait long to get ready to set up a base, as we held meetings with Osama.

Osama, as I expected, and what the President did not expect, politely told us, Hell No. After getting Russia out of the country, he was not about in anyway allow us to move in. The President was in an outrage and felt that he was had been taken advantage of and was being disrespected after all we had done to help him. However, I saw him as someone who was a lot smarter than others who foolishly accepted us as their ally.

From that day on, Osama was no longer look at as a friend or ally, but a traitor and a terrorist as far as the United States of America was concern.

It seen as some as, the dog biting the hand that fed it. They should have listen to the Colonel, and now after all that money, many felt that they had mud thrown in their face. Yet, I saw it another way, for the most important thing was that Russia was no longer in the Middle East.

So, it should not have surprised anyone when the White House knew that the jig was up on accusing Saddam for 911, they then just turned and put the blame on the old Devil himself, Osama Bin Laden. They needed someone to blame, now that all over the world people were finding out that Saddam Hussein had nothing to do with it.

The U.S. government now had someone else to blame. They knew how much they had turned the country against Osama, how much we were taught to hate him. He was a perfect scapegoat to use to stop the American from looking at the plain evidence and realizing who really did it. It looked like by now by placing the blame on Osama, now everything was going to be all right.

Well, not exactly, because now that the American people knew, uh allegedly knew, that Osama was the one who attacked us. However, with the still high cost of oil, the lifting of the Iran sanctions was back on the table. It seemed that after all that trouble they went through, they were right back to where they started.

Our intelligence over in Afghanistan did not take long to inform us that Osama had nothing do with the 911 attack, just like Saddam had nothing to do with it. So, the President ordered the air force to go over to Afghanistan and drop a few bombs along the mountainsides.

While those bombs were just designing new landscape decoration, the White House was busy coming up with a new plan to stop it lifting of the Iraq sanctions.

I remember someone in intelligence saying, what in the hell are they going to do next, blow up the White House and accuse Saddam of that? Well, fortunately, they did not blow up the White House, but it did not take them long to come up with another plan to stop the lifting of the sanctions.

They knew that they did not have much time and that they had to move fast to prevent the lifting of the Iraq sanctions. It did not take them long to move away quickly from the 911 disaster to...the Mushroom Cloud.

The White House once again, contacted it crony reporters and contacted the major owners of the media and started their new release of lies. As the televisions and radios all over the country was plastered with information that now Saddam Hussein had not attacked the United States but was getting ready to blow the U.S. off the map.

If the 911 lies against Saddam was not bad enough, by accusing him of this, they out did themselves. They were desperate enough to do anything to stop the lifting of the sanctions. Somehow, mysteriously somehow, they expected to convince the American people that Saddam now had Weapons of Mass Destruction. Soon our whole country would be just a big mushroom.

It was so crazy that you had to laugh, but unbelievable as it was and totally ridiculous, with the help of the media, they were able to trick the American people again. I remember when it happened I turn to the people in our meeting and said...Drugs, it must be all the drugs in our country, everyone is high or totally out of their mind.

The President stood before the American people and said that you have only forty-eight hours before you all will be dead, and we must attack him now.

People and few honest new medias who was actively checking into 911, now was worried that they would soon be blown into smithereens. As ridiculous as it sounded, it worked and now once again the United States were at war with Iraq.

Did the American people once again forget Desert Storm? If this man had WMDs, believe he would have used them, when we were attacking his country. Since Desert Storm, we have had him in tight surveillance, we had not only our intelligence groups over there, but the United Nations inspectors have been over there since the war.

Also, any fool would know that you don't attack a country that has WMDs. Why do you think we have not attacked North Korea? Because we think, only think that they might have WMDs and I assure you that is the only reason why we have not attacked them.

Yet, as crazy as it sounded, the American somehow ate it up, not only sucked every strip of meat off the bone but drunk it up to the very last drop and licked the bowl.

I just could not believe it, that they would even try such a stupid thing and worst of all, the American people went for it like sheep falling off a cliff. I will never understand it?

The United Nations were just as shocked as we were, the head of the United Nations spoke out against this invasion. However, after a call from the White House, he suddenly became a mute.

How could the Americans believe this, even if they did not know about the heavy intelligence surveillance that we had in Iraq. They knew that we had the U.N. inspectors over there since the war and never had anyone say anything about any WMDs.

After Desert Storm the U.N. inspectors have looked everywhere for any kind of weapons and after all these years they found nothing. Now, suddenly, the President of the United States with his binoculars see enough WMDs to turn our country into a mushroom. Before the American had time to ask, how is that possible, the President quickly move military forces into Iraq and the new Iraq war was started.

The U.N inspectors on the ground who knew this was complete nonsense. The President told that they had 48 hours to get out or if any missiles goes off course and strike them, the U.S. will not be responsible. The U.N knew that something crazy was going on, but they did not know why...we did.

Missiles being launched from all directions, most of them Tomahawks which was more like firing an oversize fourth of July candlestick rocket. The missiles were old dilapidated and should have been discarded years ago due to it exploding even before it got near its target.

Everyone knew that those lousy stale missiles would not have any effect and that a ground war was due. It was a chance to get rid of a lot of old stuff and then have the taxpayers paid to replace it with new stuff.

Finally, it seemed that they had won, after their original plan of 911 fell through, they quickly came up with Plan B, the lies of weapons of destruction, which was more unbelievable than Plan 1. At least plan 1 was something that we had done before, only we did it in other countries to start a coup or war.

Soon to carry out step 2 of Plan B they stormed into Iraq. Destroying worse than Genghis Khan, however, not in search of any WMDs but for Saddam himself, so that we could take him out and put in our own puppet regime. The plan that was created many years ago before Desert Storm was now finally being carried out.

It did not take long for the President to unroll a banner, letting the world know... Mission Accomplish. Most American was surprised at the banner being displayed when the war was still going on and countless lives were yet to be taken.

However, the mission was accomplished, not the end of a victorious war, let alone finding any WMDs. For the mission was only about getting the United States to not lift the sanctions and it had been accomplished and the Saudis read the banner before the Americans did.

However, at that time when the banner was unrolled, the White House had no idea how long this staged war would last, let alone the effect that it would have not only in America, but all around the world.

This war which many thought would be shorter than the Desert Storm conflict, but instead it has outlasted the Vietnam war. This war still goes on while I am writing this document and the sad part is that the biggest effect is yet to come.

Chapter Three

Everyone knew that 911 was Plan A and that when Plan A failed, the Lies of Weapons of Mass Destruction was Plan B. The big question to this day, that I am always asking myself is how in the world were they able to get away with it. I guess it is always easier for one to prevent a mistake than it is for one to correct it.

Even after the American people found out that there were no WMDs, they still allow the war to go on. It just showed you how much the country has changed. I remember how the people reacted to the long-lasting war of Vietnam. How they protested all over the country in the streets, across college campuses and even marched upon the White House.

How fast things have changed. Even after finding out that we have been tricked into a war. A battle that was causing the death of not only innocent Iraqis, but also America's boys and girls. Still the American people, unlike the generation before them, saw nothing wrong with allowing this horror to continue.

I ask myself what has happen to us, what apathy do we have for life and total disregard for humanity. For us to allow this war to continue after finding out that our own government lied to our faces, yet we still allow for it to go on. Have we reach a point in this country where only our own well-being matters and the life and death of other is null and void?

Do we no longer care for our Americans who are dying and losing arms and legs while we allow the war to continue. Not to mention the mental effect that it is having on so many who have come back. Do we even know the number of soldiers who have committed suicide because of the horrible things that our gov't made them do.

I remember reading in an article that an average of twenty veterans a day take their lives. Twenty veterans a day, more than the number that dies in battle. Due to the horror that we the American people placed upon them by not demanding an end to this war, like we did with Vietnam.

If the American people back then did not protest and march all over the country risking their jobs and lives, the Vietnam war would probably still be going on today. Even worst it may have escalated into a World War III, which I fear is what will soon happen. If the citizens of this country do not stand up to our corrupt money hungry establishment who create wars, not for any democracy or justice, but only for money and greed.

Unfortunately, today, sadly there is a new style of American Citizens who have no sympathy for even their fellow man or woman.

A new American that only thinks of himself and do not care the slightest for humanity or even justice when it comes to another fellow human being.

It is a sad day for America, a country that once pride itself for justice, liberty, and morality. Yet, now it is a country that sit silently as it allows its own government to wreak horror and tyranny all over the word.

With no regret, not a single bit of remorse as more and more countries are ravaged by our arm forces. Not in the name of democracy, but in the name of blatant imperialism and world domination.

No, I like many others who cannot be forgiven for the horrors and evil torturing on humanity. Which we have brought forward or allow to remain in our ungodly presence. There will be, and I ask not, for no mercy on my soul.

As we continue investigating what in the hell was going on, it kept leading us back to the White House. All the false information that was being leaked to the press, all was coming from the White House's press staff. No one seemed to even be interested in questioning it.

Has common good democracy in our gov't dissolved so much that we were about to let the lies continue like a vicious cancer and just ignore it like we thought it was the truth. I was so shocked at how the Congress in both houses would not stand up to prevent what was happening. When they all knew that it was all lies.

Is this what our democracy has come to, a gov't that now turns it back to the welfare of its people in return for monetary gain.

Only later did I find out how many members of Congress was involved. Either financially, directly or most hidden indirectly with the Middle East.

So many had invested so much money in the Middle East, that they would do anything to prevent a downfall of Saudi Arabia. Especially, since it would cause them to lose money and for some all their life savings.

Soon afterwards the intelligence came back on the number of Congressional Members So many had ties to the financial and structure building evolution in Saudi Arabia. I soon realize that this was not just a closed party of the White House, but a much, much bigger gala.

It did not take us long to conclude that there was nothing that we could do. While we helplessly sat back and saw the Iraq and Afghanistan physically and morally destroyed before our own eyes. They were going to make sure that nothing happened to Saudi Arabia's oil production and sells to the United State.

Not because they care anything for Saudi Arabia, but due to all the investments through secret corporations that they had place into the economy of the country.

I remember back then, when the weapons of mass destruction first came out in the news. I knew they had to come up with something quick to take the American minds off 911 and who was behind it.

Yet, with the U.N over there for years, I expected for someone to say, why didn't the U.N. inspectors find the weapons, if they exist?

I thought back about the Nixon's Watergate scandal and how we then had a media that was about truth and justice that allowed the people to know what was going on. Unfortunately, a time that has now been forgotten and faded through time as we have allowed large conglomerates take over the media. Who work for profits and government favors instead of the rights of the American people to know the truth.

The media which is controlled by a few giant owners quickly sided with the government to spread whatever lies needed to prevent the rich investors from losing their money. Without any concerns about how many poor American lives maybe wasted to carry it out. Yet, what is even worse is that the American people fell for it hook, line, and sinker.

I remember us asking ourselves what can we do, what should we do? Not only did many rich investors, who I might add. ones that had donated millions to just about every congressman's election. Not only that many Congress people also had invested, but even the government had taken out enormous loans from Saudi Arabia.

So, I finally convinced myself that even if it was wrong, it was necessary. However, I was not able to convince myself of this until I met with the General, who I found out was also part of it, unwillingly I must add.

After hearing that our air force was taking to the air and an all open missile-attack had been approved by all the heads of the military. It did not take me long to rush down to see the General. I rushed past his secretary and went straight into his office, madder than hell.

As I busted into his office, he had two other gentlemen in there with him. I was filled with total anger and hollered,

"General, what in the hell is going on?" He quickly excused the people from the office as he closed the door behind them. I harshly spoke to him saying, is it true that you are part of this? Did you give them the go head?

All these years, you have been the only one who have been able to prevent this? Those war hawks have been trying to start this shit in the Middle East for years. Why haven't you spoken out and stopped this?

As the General slowly returned to his chair looking down across his desk, as I continued. I shouted, "You ended Desert Storm, you prevented the President from invading Korea?" "You have always protected the people of the Middle East from these wars mongering imperialistic bastards, and now I hear that you have approved this".

I finally stopped for a moment to take a breath. That when I noticed the look on the General's face. I saw tears in his eyes as he just looked across the room and would not look my way. I then realized that somehow, somehow after all these years, they had finally gotten to him.

I stood there in silence looking at him as he just stared off and I knew then that there was no way for anyone to stop what was about to happen. I started to feel tears forming in my eyes as I stared at him. I saw tears running down his cheeks that he did not even bother to wipe off.

I stood there as my own tears started to fall, looking at the man I had admired, the man I felt was the strongest man in the world. As I realized after all these years that he stood up to them, somehow, they had broken him?

I wanted to say something, condone him in some way, but I knew there was nothing that I could say. As I turned and walked toward the door slowly opening it and walking out. Turning around to close it and take one final look at him as I slowly closed the door.

I never got the full story, but it turned out that it had something to do with his family. Something about a food for weapons type of program where his son had been set up. I knew that how they worked, if they can't get to you they then will go after your family.

I later found out that the General had a meeting with the President. He informed the President that he was through serving him and if he is re-elected that he needs to find a replacement. I cannot blame the General, no more than I can blame myself. No matter, how much I keep telling myself that by walking away like he did was not enough.

The General had clout and the President even knew that not only Congress, but the American people respected him more than they did the President. Many saw him as a future candidate for the White House. Yet, now, unfortunately, for the American people that will never be.

So often in life, we think back, what if, if we had spoken up how many lives could have been saved? Would they had just came up with something else to carry out their imperialistic desires? If we had did something, could it had made things worse and possibly a World War III?

I guess in life, we will never know? Just like back then we did not have any idea just how far this would go. I am sure that we both hoped and thought that it would be a quick and short war like Desert Storm. However, at the time we had no idea what the real plan was.

Most of the American people now, had put 911 behind them. They were content to believe what the government had told them. The media had done their part in turning the American people's eyes away from 911. They now had their eyes set on finding the WMDs so that the government would be able to prevent the mushroom cloud.

As more intelligence came in, we discovered from oversea that Saddam Hussein had asked to give himself up. To prevent an invasion that would imminently end with him being captured. That would hurt and destroy the lives of thousands of innocent Iraq citizens. Not to mention the huge destruction of buildings, homes, and valuable museums and sacred historical sites.

What a fool? Nobody wanted him, they could have easily had sent a team in to kill him long ago. This invasion had nothing to do with him, it had to do with disabling his country.

If he surrendered, then once again, we would be in the same mess as before or worse. Surely, if we allowed him to surrender than the American people would say, well now that he is gone, let us lift the sanctions and start buying cheaper Iraq oil.

This is not what we wanted. We needed to make sure that the American people would never get his cheap oil, so we could continue making huge profits off the over-priced Saudi oil. There was no way we could allow Iraq to remain intact. To prevent a great loss to not only Saudi Arabia, but to the many rich investors who have put money into Saudi Arabia.

Who knew that, if the American people were buying their oil it was a sure thing that they would get their money back with a high interest on the investment.

However, if now due to the lifting of sanctions, a cheaper price oil will be available, the government knew that it had to stop Iraq oil through any mean necessary. We had to invade Iraq and disable it and put someone in who would not try to put the cheap oil on the market.

Poor Saddam do not understand that the reason that we had to invade was not because of him, because he did not do anything, he had no WMDs. The reason that we were invading was to get the American people to turn away from asking who did 911? The best way to do that is with a war. Also, of course stop the American people from seeking cheaper oil in Iraq.

We knew that with any investigation, it would not take long for the American people to figure out that just like Saddam, Osama Bin Ladin also did not have anything to do with 911.

We had to move quickly before anyone leaked out that there were not WMDs. Especially the U.N. who knew there were no WMDs, but just like Congress, we had them in our pocket. We quickly made our move, before the media could start questioning them and one of them might break.

So, we had given the United States people another scapegoat, Mr. Ladin for 911, but we still had not achieved what we thought 911 would achieved, an excuse to invade and stop America from buying cheaper Iraq oil over the high price of Saudi oil.

So, we immediately rushed into this war, not realizing how long it was going to last, let alone how many would die. Who cares, how long it last or how many people dies if the rich investors in this country did not lose their investments over in Saudi Arabia?

Later they would lie and say they was doing it for democracy or because Saddam gassing people over thirty years ago, with the gas that we provided for them to do it with. No, it was simply because 911 did not go as planned so we had no other choice than to go to plan B, the lies of WMDs.

We could not just remove Saddam, but we had to remove also his military and government. In order, to make sure that we would be able to stop Iraq oil from being bought, we had to do an all-out war. Only by putting a puppet regime in place, would it assure that we would be able to prevent the oil from flooding the market at a cheap price.

At the time, a weak country like Iraq, after bombing the hell out of it, doing bomb raids. Knocking out communication, water, and networks across the country and blowing up building structures and homes, plus countless innocent lives. The military assured the President that it would not take but six months at most.

We knew what kind of military they had from fighting with them during Desert Storm, so the military felt it would be like taking candy from a baby. We would have them crying and surrendering in no time.

With our superior fire power, high tech weapons, superior tanks, jets, bombers, apache helicopters, superior ground troop, those backward clowns did not stand a chance. The world greatest power against those measly desert rats, everyone thought that this takeover would not take long at all.

Once we have installed a new puppet regime, we could use Iraq as a home base. We could build up our military base and later gradually advance into the surrounding countries of the Middle East.

As years started to past instead of a few months, we realize it was taking a lot longer than expected. The White House had changed hands and because the new President was elected on the stand that he was against the war and one of the few who voted against it.

Many including myself was surprised when he did a surge and sent even more troops in and escalated the war. Politicians, why should it surprise us? As, time went on, the regime was set up, but unfortunately, the war was far from
being over.

We had troops occupying Iraq and Afghanistan, we were trying to create a new military to replace the old one. However, the training was not going too well. It was not that they were untrainable, but they really did not feel that is was all right for fellow Iraqis to be killing one another. Especially, when they were being traitors, siding with the invaders who had destroyed their way of life.

While the war continued, back in the United States, unlike during Vietnam, the news did not report daily the fighting, let alone showed active fighting or even body-bags being brought back into the country.

The young people were not protesting on campuses or asking for the war to end.

As far as 911, there were only a few who questioned or seen even interested in finding out the truth and just accepted Osama as our enemy or whatever the government told them.

The media protected the government, unlike it did back in the 1970s. After a while most citizens just forgot that a war was still going on. The media that spread all over the media the lies of WMDs and got America to go into this war, now was being silent about the killings and that the war was still going on.

Especially, after the leaks about the torturing and waterboarding that the government was doing to the Iraqi people. Only a few cried out for a 911 investigation, but most seemed to accept whatever the government said.

It seems that the White House had pulled it off since after a few years less and less conspiracy theories were released. Eventually, the truth about the WMDs reluctantly came out and was soon broadcasted across the nation that there were no WMDs. However, the American people did not get too upset about being lied to. For no one demanded an end or even protested as the war just continued for years.

Even the White House was surprised at the way the country showed such apathy toward the war. Maybe because of all the violence on tv, they no longer saw war is wrong like we did during Vietnam?

The President expected that the people would demand an end to the war, because it had gone on longer than anyone expected. However, it seems that the American people were not outraged by the government lying to them.

Very soon more contractors were over in Iraq than soldiers, and with everything being taken over by the Westerners, this only made more upset Iraq citizens to join different protesting armies and radicals.

They quickly realized that they were not being liberated but colonized by the powerful westerners who now was running everything.

With 911, we came up with a scapegoat Bin Laden, but for the WMDs we did not have a scapegoat, but it turns out that to the American people, we did not need one. Was it because we were a Christian society and we were killing Muslims, so they did not care?

It seems that the American people really did not care, they did not care about the hundreds of thousands of Muslims lives that were being destroyed, let alone the thousands of Americans and allies. During these long years, many lives have been wasted and millions had to run from the war and become poor desperate refugees.

The morals of justice, kindness, peace seeking, and caring seems to be something of the past for America. As the war continued and more people died due to lies from our government, but America did not care. The media did not bring it into their living rooms or now days should I say family rooms, and then it was a foreign war that did not concern them.

America views on war had greatly changed and changed unfortunately for the worst. Instead of a country that once fought war only to obtain peace or to stop others from torturing and dominating a country like we did in the past.

Now, we saw our government being the imperialistic dictator doing a takeover of a country. Something that we once despised of any other country doing to another.

It now seems that we have become a country like Germany where a dictator like Hitler was welcome. Just like the people of Germany who ignored or did not care when Hitler was murdering millions of innocent Jewish people. Now, we were doing the same while the American people just ignored it just like the German people did. What is that old saying, history repeats itself. I wonder if this war will last long enough until WWII will repeat itself as well.

We allow money hungry greedy capitalists to control our government and take away our democracy and idea of freedom for all. As we saw them replace it with a fascist imperialistic regime of world domination. This country of our has changed completely from the way it was forty years ago.

As the war continued and increased in force, while it decreases in the news and in the minds of the people, no one saw any end in sight. It was like a war that was not reality, that was not going on. More like a reality show when the few times that the news media mention that a few soldiers died or that our government bombed a new location.

Usually, they only did that when they knew that it was being reported in other countries news and due to the internet, they would report it before it showed up on YouTube or talked about in some international chat room.

Also, every so often, the news would report that our military had taken over a part of the country or had retaken an area that they had lost. Just to make the American people think that we were victorious and winning the war.

Just lies and more lies, just like the lies of WMDs that got us into this long lasting unjust war. As the war continued, finally they were successful at finding Saddam. A jack legged jury and court was quickly put in place that resembled a 1900 southern court in the deep south.

The kind of court having an all-white KKK jury and the judge the imperial grand wizard. With a black man being charged, no matter what he was being charged with, we all knew that outcome before the trail even started.

I have seen this happen so many times before and so many times afterwards, just like Gadhafi, it does not matter if they convict you in a court or even in the streets. The verdict is always the same, where you are assumed guilty with no chance of being proven innocent. Gadhafi was murdered not because of those who tried for years to present him as a tyrant.

Once again, it was all about the money. As he tried to build up the African countries by them creating their own financial structures of banks to loan to their countries instead of using western banks.

The western banks were not about to let that happen and they called on their political power houses, who they had bought and own, to put a stop to it. Which they did right away before the American people even knew the military was in Libya.

This time everything went as planned and before anyone knew what was going on, Gadhafi was dead, and we had moved out. Letting the people rise in any form of chaos as groups fought for leadership. One can only give this move 5 stars in quick execution, job completion, and quick exit. This is a perfect example of how operations are supposed to go.

I often wondered what went through Saddam' mind as he sits there in the courtroom having an unjust trial by enemies. He knew the whole thing was a waste, because he knew his verdict before the trial even started.

I guess that they could not just cut off his head or beat him to death where they found him. Like what happened to Gadhafi, since the news reported that he had been found by an American soldier in a hole.

A man who had for years been an ally of ours, a man who went against the welfare of his own people for us. A man who thought of us as brothers, now he was having his own people who now are our puppets, taking him out. Did this fool believe in us so much that he thought that he might be put in an American jail in luxury and later released?

I cannot understand his thinking. I have asked myself so many times, why didn't he see this coming? It was only years later that I found out that he had been lied to by us. He was told that just like old boy Noriega, we were going to look after him.

He was told that he was only going to have to do a little time in a nice disclosed private prison and after good behavior be able to live the rest of his life in a blissful retirement.

I guess when they slipped that rope around his neck, he realized in this business, you can't trust anyone. Saddam was no fool, if you think that he was not smart, or not as smart as you, then why aren't you a leader of a country?

No one who is stupid can become a leader of a country, let alone run a country. However, even the smartest can be fooled and lied too. I am sure if he had a chance to do it over again, he would have left the country before the first U.S. plane flew over. With all that money of his, some country would had accepted him and not extradite him.

Even when he had the chance to put a stop to this at the beginning. They assured him that he would be taken well care of. I am sure if he had any notion that we would betray him, and he would end up dead, he would have "Bet On RED."

"Bet On RED", is slang term that we started using after the country of Cuba became communist. Back then when the Bay of Pig operation failed miserably, and it became a big embarrassment to the President as well as to the country. The President realized that Fidel Castro had a little bit more muscle than we had expected.

It was the worst embarrassment of it times. A powerful country like ours sent in our highly trained professional troops and they are taken out by a rag tag untrained militia. What an embarrassment.

We thought that once they saw our troops, they would jump on their knees and surrender. At least that is how it always happens in the movies. When the cavalry coming in blowing their horn, you know the battle is over.

Somehow, for some strange reason it did not work out that way. Our troops were marched on public television with their hands up as a rag style military with all smiles marched them back down to their ships.

The President did not waste any time to make sure that did not happen again. As the military prepare for an all-out war starting with bombing the hell out of them before any more of our troops were sent in.

Fidel Castro has some sense, he knew he got lucky with the first small ground invasion, but the next ground strike and the air bombardment, he knew he had no chance in hell of surviving it. The White House gave him one choice and that was to surrender at once.

We were sure that he would do the right thing and surrender. He could not be stupid enough of thinking of taking us on. Knowing that all he would be doing is killing his own people before we took over his country. He knew that this time we meant business with no holds barred.

No one had any idea that instead of surrendering, which seemed to be the only available choice that he had. Instead be beat us again, by contacting the Soviets and joining the Communist to prevent us from attacking his country.

Saddam was no fool, he saw how it had worked for Cuba, he knew it would have worked for him. However, the White House was able to convince him that he would be well taken care of. He would end up with billions of dollars and just like with the Philippines, where President Ferdinand Marcos was taken care of the same would happen to him.

The White House knew by promising him this that he would just sit and wait. Until they flew in a private helicopter or plane to sweep him out of the country before the missiles started lightening up the skies. Oh, say can you see by the dawn early lights, twilight gleaming, rockets busting in air. I just wonder what went through his mind when that helicopter never showed up.

I don't mean to laugh, for God knows that it was not right, it was wrong, so wrong. After all he did for us over the years and after they did it for Marcos. I am not sure why they allowed for him to die. I guess it had to have been personal. Some people just carry a grudge.

I wonder why they gave the stupid forty-eight-hour deadline before the attack. Maybe, they asked him how long it would take for him to pack and he said a day or two. Heh, heh, heh, I don't mean to be funny, I have seen so many die from lies, that there is nothing funny about it.

After the death of Saddam, the Iraq war and Afghanistan war continued. We all thought that it would end now, that Saddam was dead, and our puppets were all put in place. However, we did not count on the freedom fighters, as I like to call them, the good old boys.

Even after we had destroyed Saddam's military and now had our puppet military in place being trained. That is another joke, we had no need to train them because we were not planning on leaving anytime soon. We use that is an excuse to remain over there. Everything was going well as planned, except for what we did not expect, "the good old boys."

I like to call them the good old boys, like the guys we have here who drive around in pickup trucks. Showing off the flag and believing in their rights to bear arms. If

Russia was ever able to take down our military, I feel these same old good old boys, would rise to the occasion, and keep the war going.

Our government may like to refer to them as terrorist. They are no more terrorist than the Native Americans who stood up fighting for this country when the white man invaded. No more terrorist than Nat Turner when he started to kill his oppressor to obtain his freedom. To me, these men, women, and children are freedom fighters trying to remove their oppressors.

The same oppressors that back in the thirties that came about wreaking havoc in European countries as Nazism spread across the globe. Just like I would hope every red-blooded American would stand and fight for this country if anyone try to take it, or change our way of life, liberty, and the pursuit of happiness.

One man's terrorist, is another man's freedom fighter. For any country, be it the United States or any other, is invaded for whatever reason, be it lies of WMDs, or else should be proud to fight and die for their country to protect the way of life that they love.

Due to these freedom fighters, the Iraq and Afghan war continued. While these wars were going on there was a push for us to go into Iran. However, due to these freedom fighters and especially due to the fighters in Syria, it was put off.

It was still a rumor that they had WMDs, but the White House felt that they did not and wanted to attack Iran. Due to those of us who felt there was a possibility of them having WMDs, and with the civil fighting going on, we won the argument not to invade Iran, at this time.

I and other argued that if Iran did not have any WMDs, I am sure that if we started a war with them that they would not hesitate to "Bet on Red."

Our relationship with Russia was not all that great and Russia was upset over the invasion into the Middle East, especially since no WMDs were found and the war was still going on. So luckily, we did the right thing and did not invade the country of Iran but placed it into Plan Phase Two.

Since the plan to go into Iran fell through, then the White House wanted to discuss an invasion into North Korea, which surprised me because there was a 50/50 chance that they had WMDs. After arguing with the White House, then they came up with putting more bases into South Korea. Even when the people of South Korea felt that there were already too many bases there now.

Of, course the reason that we had so many bases over there in South Korea was so that it we were ever able to start a coup in North Korea, we could very easily move in quickly and take down the North Korea military and then make the country as Korea as it was originally.

Speaking of a coup, the coup of all coups, came forward at the end of 2012. It had taken years for us to set up our cells all over several specific countries. Why wait around doing one at a time when you could save so much time by setting off several at the same time. By doing this other country would not have time to try to get involved with some other country uprising if they had one of their own going on at the same time.

They decided that the name that would be given to this multi coup uprising would be called "Arab Spring". As we all know how Hitler started with the European countries when he started his quest to rule the world. Napoleon chose France, Spain, and Italy to start it world conquest.

Could it be something instilled in all of us, going back to the reign of the Roman Empire or even before. Is there something in our DNA or is it something morally behavioral learned that cause us to want to dominate another.

To overpower a fellow human being to show our dominance. I am not sure, but it does appear that there is always someone, somewhere, at some time that is always doing it.

The "Arab Spring" was set up by what I will refer to only as the Secret Society. Which many may not have ever heard of or at least do not believe really exist. No one including myself knows when it first came about. Many can only guess at who the key players are.

The so-called Secret Society do not only control our political leaders, but also have control of the money that is used across the world. I guess when you able to practically control all the world's monetary structure, you might as well next try to control the people as well. If for no other reason just to make sure that your money is safe.

The "Arab Spring" was set up as a multi-faceted coup that would start out into two phases. The first phase was to consist of the following countries..., Tunisia, Egypt,

Libya, Syria, Yemen, Bakrin, Kuwait, Lebanon, Oman, Morocco, Jordan, Sudan, Mauritania, and Saudi.

Even with Iraq and Afghan war still going on and lasting a lot longer than expected. The Secret Society informed the main ring leaders of the political arena that it was time to make the move. Probably, they felt it was necessary to move now because of what was happening with Gadhafi with the banking and financial structure. Also, due to the long war, there were some who was now viewing the United States more of an oppressor than a liberator.

It worked out well in Libya, as Gadhafi after ruling his country for forty-two years was finally taken down. For forty-two years he remained in power with several attempts throughout the years were all unsuccessful. Even the one that I was personally in charge of.

Now, after all these years, he would not be killed from some western foreigner, but by the bloody hands of his own people. This was something that the SS (Secret Society) was very proud of. It was a possible boost also for the military leaders. Who now felt that one day we would have some military bases over in the country once things cool down.

Ever since Gadhafi came into power and closed the United States Wheelus Air Force Base, along with the British bases, he became number one on America's shit list. Now the United States after so many years was finally having its revenge.

Many other countries of the multi-faceted coup were being successful even if not as well as Libya, a lot of their leaders were ousted. Others like Egypt, Yemen, and other was not quite as successful, or should we say, at least not yet.

The one that really put a snag into the "Arab Spring" was Syria. Who would have thought it? One that we thought would fall quickly instead put up a hell of a fight. The war is still going on strong and worst of all, now Russia is getting involved.

We saw that the coup was failing even after we sent more weapons to the protestors and radicals. Even after sneaking in more of our own troops under cover, we realized that this guy was intending to be the last Mohican. He had no plans of releasing his country.

When over a year had gone past, the President received a strong stern request form the Secret Society to get it over with now. So, we reinforced and supplied better weapons, but still that damn Bashar Al-Assad would not surrender. He just kept fighting and fighting and eventually, it seems that he had a good chance at surviving.

This of course was not good news for the Secret Society. It seems that the only way that we would be able to take him out is if we got involved with our air power. We could bomb a path for the protestors to overthrow him.

The decision was made, and it was up to the White House to come up with an excuse for our air attacks to go in. It was suggested at first that we would use the same old lies of WMDs. Eventually, we persuade the President that we got away with it once, let us at least wait a little longer before we try that one again. We had to come up with something and we had to come up with it quick.

Assad was winning the war and instead of him surrendering, we were getting reports that the radicals were thinking about surrendering because of the high fatalities.

This is when someone remembered about the toxic gas that we and Britain gave to them to use against their neighbors. We now had ourselves a fool proof plan to invade the country or at least a cause to bomb the hell out of it so that the rebels could later come in and take it over.

Our plan was simple, we would just say that the Syrian government was illegally using toxic gas in the war against the rebels. It was much better than the lies of WMDs in Iraq, because we knew for sure that Syria had the toxic gas.

All we had to do is a little acting for the cameras. Go to where there were some rebels coming back wounded from the war and say that we found toxic gas on them. Just to make it look even better we could even involve some children being sprayed by the gas.

The plan looked so simply, that I myself and everyone else knew that it would surely work. Not only the U.N., but the whole world would not be able to fault us for attacking Syria, after they started poisoning innocent civilians. We did the filming and got it out to the international news and sure enough it fooled everybody, except... for Putin.

The President of Russia, who just happen to have a good intelligence force just like us. His intelligence quickly assured him that those toxic gases that were given to Assad, had been packed away years ago and never even opened.

Putin put his name up and called out our bluff. He even went as far as contacting the Syrian President and talked him into allowing the toxic gas to be removed to show to the world that he never used the toxic gas that we and Britain gave him in hopes of him using it against his neighbor countries.

The President of Russia was tired of people getting killed over lies and finally had enough and was standing up to the United States. He not only guarantees that Syria had never used any toxic gases, but now he was standing up in support of the Assad government. Putin told the U.S. and the U.N. they could come in and not only check for themselves, but also remove all the toxic gas that were given to Assad.

Our brilliant plan to finally put this war away and to take out Assad had just exploded in our face. Now, not only did the plan not work and prove to many that we were still good at lying.

It also has gotten Putin to step up and now we knew that with Putin in the picture it was going to be harder than hell to achieve what we wanted. Not only that, but with two top leaders on opposite side we just hoped that it would not escalate into a World War. The President felt that it was time now to start ending the war. The Secret Society said...No!

Unfortunately, the war did not end, Assad did not blink and our support for the Radicals even with now Russia in the game continued, but at a slower pace. Eventually, as the war continued, it only got worse for us and the innocent Syrian people.

Due to the chaos from the war, the country became more dismantling as the stability of the country got worse. Creating starvation, homelessness, and refugees running for the border trying to get away from it all.

However, I believe sooner or later, it will fall and the other countries as well. For one day, maybe later than expected we will be able to start Phase II. Believe me America, Imperialism is alive and well.

Many people, not only in the United States, but all over the world, and especially in Muslim countries wondered if what is going on in the Middle East was a Holy War? Is it or could it possibly be in some way a Christian Crusade against Muslim people?

As ridiculous is that may sound to many of us, it is not like this has never happened. We all remember the Holocaust, when the people of Germany had a blind eye to what their government was doing in other countries. Not realizing that millions of innocent Jewish people were being massacred.

The Christian Crusades were religious wars that took place between the eleventh and fifteenth century. In 1095 Pope Urban II called for attacks on Muslims and to conquers their land which they considered the Holy Land. Many did not see it as a religious thing as much as an economic financial gain which is what most wars are based on.

Killing and pillaging across the land, massacring thousands of not only Muslims but also Jews. Anyone who was not a Christian or who would not conform into the Christian belief were murdered and exterminated by the order of the Church. The sands of the Middle East were soaked with blood, the same way that they are being soaked today due to the

United States' lies of weapons of mass destruction.

Many around the world, not only Muslims have asked that once the United States citizens found out that their government lied to them about the WMDs, why have they allowed this war to continue. Why are they invading surrounding countries and destabilizing them all over the Middle East? It is easy to see how Muslims could easily see this is another modern day Holy War against their religion.

I myself feel that this may be true to some degree, those who are called Religious Rights, or extreme Christians. However, I feel the majority who are behind this is not due to any religious reason, just as I feel the Christian Crusade may have started out due to religion but continue centuries later because of greed and wealth.

I believe that any country that believes in God, would not sit back and allow hundreds of thousands of God's children to be massacre once they found out that there were no WMDs. However, maybe most in this country do not see them as God's children. They do not see them as they see themselves.

I will not say that our country is racist, but I ask you, did you see black people is God's children when we kidnapped them and put them into slavery. Did we see the Native Americans as our fellow God's children as we massacred them and stole their land? Many who did it in the name of religion.

However, if you say that we are not racist, I feel that at least you must say that we are prejudice. Just look at World War II, the first thing that comes to one's mind as soon as we say WWII is Adolf Hitler.

The Germans who tried to take over the world. The awful Nazi who we cannot stand, not only for the war they started, but also for the killing of so many Jewish people.

We may say that Hitler was a terrible, terrible tyrant, yet it was not Hitler or the Germans that we dropped the Atomic Bomb on. They were the cause of the war, they were the ones taking over other countries, the one who murdered the Jewish people, but we did not drop the bomb on them.

Going by our American history book, it will tell you that the bomb was finalize after Hitler and Germany gave up. Yet, it was available two years before the Nazi surrendered.

We decide to drop the bomb on a darker skin people, not the white skin German who started all of this. All the terror that the Nazi did, this country could not see us drop an atomic bomb on our fellow white people.

Yet, they not only dropped one atomic bomb, but two atomic bombs on the darker skin Japanese. You may disagree with me as you like, you may say that America is total non-racist and have never been racist, that is your opinion and your choice.

America citizens are strange, during the elections some will decided who their leader of this country will be solely based on their religious view on abortion. While at the same time they will elect a President, who has killed thousands of people in a war.

All throughout history, many wars have been fought over religious reasons. As some would say in the name of God! I myself do not believe that God want war. God does not side with anyone who promote war over peace, let alone is God anyone's co-pilot.

Thy Shall Not Kill is what we may say in our churches, while at the same time we allow our government to slaughter people in other countries all over lies of WMDs, while we ignore the massacre and look the other way. What a Godly country we are.

Politicians are great at averting the eyes of the citizens away from the real problems of this country. We see this everywhere, if it be in religion, sex, or race. Instead of talking about problems that affect all of us such as jobs, economy, education, and real basic needs of this country.

Instead they use dirty politics, using people religious faith by saying that one is more religious than the other. They call each other bigots or racist, when both are.

The American people always fall for it, they listen to who can throw the most dirt, instead of presenting their policies to solve all the problems that we have. The American people are always falling for it, so I guess the politicians know what they are doing.

Look at the drugs in this country, do you really think that our government cannot prevent drugs in this country. Once again, do I have to remind you that we are a Capitalist country, not a Democratic one.

Drugs, it is true, are evil and destroy lives, but it is also very profitable. Very profitable, not only for the drug dealers, but for the entire country as well.

It is not only a street crime, but also a greater white-collar crime. Money laundering by banks, where banks helps themselves to a big chunk of it in return for making it legal tender on the bank's spreadsheet. They have people investing money, money that has been gain legally through hard work and honest means. The bank turns this money over to the drug dealer and get in return three times that amount which they put on the books as account receivables from the investors. No government keep track of how the money goes up or down so like Bernie Madorf, you can put down millions while receiving nothing or tens of millions.

Even after Bernie and the 2008 crash, it is still being done now more than ever, because they know that the government has their backs. The bank uses a procedure of layering drug money through transactions in different forms making it impossible for any trail to be tracked. They not only do it nationally, but also use off shore investing, third world set up financial structures to funnel money.

Using loan companies, investment corporations, car dealerships, even auctions to circulate the money back into the monetary system It is very easy for financial institutions to do this by using construction loans which made Miami and other major cities. So, there is a lot of white collar crooks who makes a great deal of money from the drug trade.

The ones who don't make much money are the poor guys on the street corner. He is the one who works hard on the street not sitting behind a desk in a bank or investment firm. He is the one that is hounded by the police and end up going to jail unlike the top dogs who have paid off government officials, so they will never have to worry about stuff like that.

America is no democracy, it was set up based on Capitalism from the day that our country was founded. It is much worst today because we allow it to be, unlike our forefathers who kept it under control. Today we the American people are allowing it to run rampant.

We have a gov't that will save the rich on Wall Street and the rich one percent. Look out for the rich billionaires instead of doing anything for the homeless poor.

Look at Walmart, a company that make million and millions of dollars and the owners are all rich billionaires. While many of the people who do all the work are living off wages that are below standard living conditions. The reason being greed, where the owner takes most of the profit and does not provide a reasonable share to its workers.

Something that has happened before especially with the Rockefellers and other rich, therefore we created unions. Yet, today the unions are quickly disappearing or losing their power due to a government that is bought and own by the rich establishment. That we, the working class and poor, allow to control our government. This is called Capitalism, where he who has the gold rule.

We are a Capitalist country and democracy is a farce. The people do not rule the country, the country is ruled by those politicians that are bought by the crooked rich establishment that we allow to run this country. Capitalist greed is what runs this country, not Democracy, let alone the American people.

The rich minority who weaken our unions and have forced the working class into accepting a minimum wage which no one is able to live on. Therefore, we have an immigration problem today.

The government for years has allowed illegal aliens from Mexico to flood our country. It benefits not only the illegal aliens, but also those who hires their labor. However, our low pay American laborers has been hurt greatly by this in many ways. They have not only lost their jobs to these illegal aliens, but also have not received an increase in the minimum wage due to them.

Those Americans who benefitted from the illegal low wage Mexican worker, did not think of what effect it would have years later. They did not have the sense years ago to realize what effect that would take on the country later.

A generation later when the children of those illegal aliens would grow up and instead of taking the poor manual worker job, now they are seeking middle class and upper-class jobs. These kids want more than a mere manual job that their parent have.

Only now, are you hearing people complaining about Mexico immigration. Take drugs, it started out with the poor white hippie style neighborhood and those who were consider anti-establishment. During a time when black people were strongly fighting for equal rights. Demanding equality and they were able to achieve it even if it took by any means necessary!

Black people in this country created a strong movement and out of it came equal rights and respect for people of color. This is when the establishment became delirious and demanded a way to come up with a plan to stop this powerful movement. Then they remembered the hippie, the foolish good guy wanted to put flowers in his hair and smoke a joint. Not caring about society, just wanting to feel good and looking for the next high.

So, we decided that would be the answer to stopping the black movement in our white country. We flooded their neighborhoods with drugs. The smart one sold it for us and the rest bought it and used it. It was a huge success and we were able to put a stop to the black power movement.

The drugs became our miracle drug, it brought crime to their former peaceful neighborhoods. The most important thing it did was to cause the loss of their dignity and respect. We no longer needed the Klu Klux Klan or any white supremacist group to stop them with. Now they were destroying each others without any help from the outside.

All over the country where we put drugs, it was a huge success. Back in the days of lynching blacks, I am not sure how many blacks died annually. I am sure that today a whole lot more of them die by their own hands than whatever number it was during Jim Crow.

Now days, it is not only keeping black down and in line, but also poor whites and other poor minorities as well. Not to even mention the money that is being made. So much money and that is why we are in the process of trying out drugs across our entire nation. If it was successful with the poor class, why not the middle class. The main reason it has not exploded in the middle class is because they are more law abiding.

This is when we thought, why don't we make it legal, so we will be able to control them too. We knew how most people viewed drugs and would never allow the federal gov't to make it legal like we did with alcohol. So, we decided to experiment with it starting with the states. Cannabis was legal in this country as used as medicine to some. We started it out as being used for medicinal purposes to test the water and then later allow each state to decide if it should be recreational.

We believe that most of these people will be anti-establishment and this way we will have a way to control them or they probably will not even care what we do to the country. I mean even today, only about fifty percent of eligible voter's vote. Imagine the power we would have if we could knock it down to just twenty percent or less.

The goal will be the same as with the black neighborhoods. Where the rich establishment will have full control of the working middle class just as they do with the poor communities. It is called power of them. The main reason that we felt it was necessary was because of what we saw happen in other countries. Countries that we had been able to pull off coups in and how easily the people were able to take out the present government.

We knew that once we were under British rule and how we led a revolution in this country and liberated the people. We knew that the same thing could easily happen again if we did not take steps so see that the Capitalist own establishment find a new way to control the people so that would not happen.

Our country was built from a revolution, so we knew that it was possible that another revolution could come about. Especially, due to the big gap that we have in this country between the have and the have nots. In a country where the rich keep getting richer while the poor gets poor.

When millionaires are becoming billionaires, while the minimum wage and weakening of unions are causing more poverty or lower class. How long before they wake up and see that their crooked government that is bought and own by the rich no longer represent them. Will next year or ten years from now will they wake up and say, we will not eat cake?

Therefore, we must start weakening the middle class, the same way we have with the poor blacks in this country. Congress will be told to turn a blind eye to the states that we experiment in and if those states pass the test then it will be implemented across the entire country. We will start it through the state government not only to make tax money off it, but mainly so we can control the potency of it.

Think of how we sell beer, in white neighborhoods, we sell only Coors, Miller, Bud, etc. While in black neighborhoods we sell Colt 45 malt liquor a more potent drink. We will have the same ability with marijuana to control the potency to the different neighborhoods. We will start off very light to get everyone to use it and then later modify it to those area that we need to control.

That is not the only thing that we are planning on doing. For if the average citizen does not have guns, it would be much harder for them to ever have a revolution against the establishment. We must work also on getting rid of guns in this country. So that only us establish militia that works for us will have guns to keep control of the 99%.

We will start getting rid of powerful rifles and automatics, once we have successfully done that we then will get rid of the rest to ensure that the people will have no means of revolutionizing against us.

This I fear will be much harder to carry out than the drugs, so we will concentrate mainly on the drugs and let the ban on guns be our secondary priority. If we can get the right people in the political arena, we can have them get rid of the Second Amendment and that is the best way to begin for now.

To whomever is reading this, and I pray that it got into the right hands. I know that I am going to bust Hell wide open. I am going to boil for eternity in the pits of Hell like a lobster in a pot or a fish at a fish fry. For I like my comrades did not speak out because we were more concerned for our own financial welfare than for the welfare of this country.

There is nothing religious or godly about us. The only thing that we have ever worshipped is the mighty dollar. I do not ask for any forgiveness, for I surely do not deserve none. I will only pray that the memories and nightmares that I have endured through the years for what we did, will along with my soul burn up in the hellish flames.

Every time I see a cripple or disabled veteran in a wheel chair or a sad soldier trying to make it in this world with false limbs. I wonder if I had spoken up, I wonder if it would have made a difference? Would it had prevented so many deaths, the pains of their love ones, the agony of their horrendous misery?

Would the American people had even listened? Would they had listen to a nobody, some stranger that they knew nothing of, over the words of a President that they trusted and elected? My mere words over the shouts of the house and senate of the Congress who they had personally picked to represent them?

I ask you, would I not have been called a liar, a fool, a madman, a kook or nut trying to get attention. Would I not have shamed my family as I am treated like a traitor and criminally prosecuted by the ones who I tried to protect them from.

I keep telling myself that I had no choice, it would have been only my few words against all of them. Why would they believe me against their government, against their country? Would they believe my mere words over that of the President's? Especially when, unlike Monica, I had no dress.

How could I have made a difference? How could I, by myself possibly in any way convince them to trust me? Someone who they do not even know, my word against theirs. When at the same time, I myself knew that the American people did not want to know the truth. They did want to force themselves to believe that a country that they thought was God forsaken and bless was instead the evils of Hell right here on earth.

Just like my friends, who names I will not reveal. Who not only alerted the American people of the lies of WMDs. They also got rid of the WMDs that they dumped on the way to Iraq, which was to be place there to prove that Iraq had WMDs. It also costed them their lives and I am sure they sacrificed their lives willing, thinking that it would put an end to the war. Yet, years later the war continued, I ask you did they do the right thing?

You tell me what they died for? What in the sense of sanity, would you give up your life when it does not change anything. If they had known that by sacrificing their lives would have the same affect is placing the WMDs in Iraq, I am sure that they would have follow the plan. Instead of trying to alert a country to the evils in our government when it is a country that does not care to know.

As I hastily write these memoirs down in hope that the American people will one day see it. I ask myself will it change anything? Have we as a country been told so many lies, we been drenched in so much corruption and outright hatred toward our fellow man. Is there any hope for us ever to become a God-fearing country again?

I think of people like those who gave up their lives, so the American people would find out about Guantanamo. The horror, suffering torture and out right slaughter that took place. Was it worth it, was it worth them dying to let the world know what our government was doing to fellow human beings who were never charged with anything.

Innocent people who had done nothing wrong, but wrongfully accuse because of bounties we place for dissidents. People turning in their innocent neighbors who they did not like, just to get money.

None of the people ever went to trial cause all evidence we had was all hearsay and countless witnesses came to their defense, but the right to a trial or innocent until proven guilty, does not exist under the Patriot Act. Many were tired of the torturing, many soldiers shot themselves in the head or committed suicide instead of being forced to torture these innocent people.

Other who survived, later after returning homes reliving the nightmares, committed suicide for what they had been forced to do. Yet, even after some came forward risking their lives taking picture and releasing it to the press, nothing changed. Yet, you have the nerve to tell me that I was obligated to say something before now?

Especially the black soldiers, I think it affected them the most. It surely bought back a past of brutality and killing that one could only compare to slavery in the early years of this country. Like the charge of the light Brigade, ask not the reason why, ask but to do or die. Obey your orders soldier or you will be in the brig beside him or maybe we will just let you die?

Did not America, see these people, or did they just see them as animals? I feel they would have care more for animals being mistreated than they were for these innocent people. After finding out about the torturing and killings, they did not rise, speak out of the injustice, they just turned a blind eye as those responsible received no punishment. Only a few innocent soldiers who were only carrying out their orders were the only ones who received any punishment at all.

I say to you if I burn, I surely will not burn alone. I do not think that I will be lonesome in Hell. I am not trying to put the blame on anyone else, but surely there is enough blame for every American citizen. Who stood silently by while we allow this horror to continue after finding out that there were no WMDs.

Even when Wiki-leaks and other sources even released information to the American people, about the wrongs of this war, they did nothing. If I truly thought that my voice would have made a difference, when so many other voices were ignored, I too would have spoken out.

Yes, I held my tongue, I held it, I ask you, would you have not done the same? I believe in patriotism as much as you but believe me I believe in God much more. As a God-fearing soul should I have spoken out? Should I had spoken out risking my life for nothing.

Would you say that I should regret that I have only one life to give for my country? Maybe, but give a life to a country that does not even care? A country that has seen so much killing not oversea, but right here in its own streets, these killings has become as common as the sun rising every day.

Have we not become a country that has placed itself into a trance or coma, having our eyes fully open, but not allowing our brain to even comprehend that which we choose not to see? What good would it had done, why do I even think that it will do some good now? When I know that the American people do not wish to hear the truth. They want to keep their eyes shut, so they can keep believing that America is great!

Even when they see how the country is changing right before them. They sit there with their hands in their laps, why they see their rights being violated and their laws being broken.  God, how can I even think that I have any chance of convincing them of what evil is going on in this country, when in their heart and soul, they do not want to know.

How can you convince someone that your enemy cannot harm you, but watch your closet friend?  That the one that you suppose to love, and I do love my country, is the one who will cut your hair and rob you of all your strength.

I know that there will be many who will not believe me.  What worst will be those who believe me, but still will not have the will to make a change.  How can I convince them that if nothing is done about 911, surely there will be another attack someday on our people.  Another attack by the hands of our government for whatever stupid or monetary reason that they come up with.

For when one gets away with doing something wrong, it only encourages one to continue to do wrong.  No matter what you may think, I have been a good loyal patriot to my country.  I can keep a secret, for I know that there are some things best for the people not to know.  Especially, when it comes to war and what one must find themselves doing to win it, even when it means the death of one's own President.

## Chapter Four

The Gulf of Tonkin Resolution lies by the military and staff that was used to get authorization for United States to start the Vietnam War. They lied about North Vietnam attacking ships of the United States. When the truth was that the Vietnamese did not attack even after the United States approached their shores hoping that they would.

The United States used the ship Maddox that was ordered to approach the shore of Vietnam expecting that the Vietnamese would shoot the ship for invading their water.

After they were not able to provoke Vietnam into attacking the ship, they then decided to create a false report to the President. The report claimed that the Vietnamese attacked the ship even after several attempts they could not get the Vietnamese to do so.

The United States military fired upon its own ship the Maddox to damage it to look like it had been fired on by the Vietnamese during a battle. They fired several shots into the ship, so it would look like a good full fledged attack upon it.

The crew then was told to claim that they were attacked by three Vietnam torpedo ships while it was in international waters.

A total absolute lie just like the lies of WMDs. You see when you get away with it once, that only encourage you to lie again and again.

They successfully staged a fake attack upon the Maddox and then created a fake report that was sent to the President. They then worked on the President, convincing him that we cannot allow them to attack us and do nothing about it.

The report including the killing of three men during the attack which was not a lie. To make sure the President would be persuaded to go into war, they felt that there need to be some casualties. If someone just fired upon the ship, it was a good chance that the President would have chosen to ignore it or just send them a letter for an apology.

As hours pass, one small lie turns into bigger lies, as later they said that it was not just one ship but two. They said the battle lasted a long time and the lies just kept growing. They said everything that they could think of to make sure that the President would go to Congress and stress the need for war.

Due to our intelligence, it did not take us long after checking the ship and talking to people we had over in Vietnam, that everything that they were saying was in error. However, the President wanted to believe his military staff and did not accept our conclusions.

I remember contacting those in Congress that knew me well. However, I was surprised at how they acted like they did not even want to see the intelligence investigation report. I remember one of them Morse, pushed for the committee to view the report, but still it was not considered. I remember how later that he was black balled and how he lost his re-election for trying to prevent the Vietnam War.

It did not take me long to realize what others had told me that to survive in this business, it is best for you to learn how to play along. You only get two choices, play along with what come down from the mountain or resign and not play at all. This is when I first realized just how much and how determine some was to get into this war at any cost and by any means necessary.

I guess in a false sense back then, I looked at it is having to do good, you must accept the bad of others, to achieve the good for many. The President and many were against the people liberation that was trying to liberate the country.

Back in the 1850s, France began a conquest of Indo-China and it was placed under the French colonial rule. Many of the Vietnamese were in opposition of the French rule. Soon they formed a Viet Nimh group that was back by the Communist to help the people to liberate themselves from the French rule and colonization.

During World War II, the Japanese invaded and because of the war, it helped the liberators to gain more power which led eventually to their long-awaited Independence. America of course, favored the French while the Soviet and China favored the liberated Vietnamese. So of course, a war was soon to come.

So, they ended up splitting the country into two parts. They used the 17th parallel line to mark the division between the two groups in the country. The country of Vietnam became the North Vietnam and South Vietnam. It did not take long before the North who did not honor outsiders dividing up their country, made their move and invaded Laos.

The United States provided guns and money to the South to defend itself against the North. It was a Civil War, one could say like the Civil War that we fought here in our own country. The only difference that our war was only among fellow citizens of the country, not outsiders from other countries.

The White House staff and mainly the generals of the military wanted to get the United States military involved. The President did not want to send America's children into a civil war that he felt should be decided by the people. Yet, he strongly believed that the country would be better off being more a Western style government than a Communist one.

The White house staff and generals fought hard trying to persuade the President that we needed to send our United States military in. As the Civil War started leaning more to a victory for the North Vietnamese, they were able to talk him into an air assault. We sent in many military advisors and more weapons as they continued to persuade the President for a full ground attack.

As time went on we started a so-called secret bombing attack on all the major North Vietnam points of where their military were being stationed.

We had a small so-called secret group of troops over there training and fighting along with the South Vietnamese, but it was not being successful. The generals and White House staff knew that the only way we could prevent the North from taking over the South was through a full ground attack which would be a war.

The President by the middle of 1963, knew that the bombing and secret troops were not working. He knew that a full out attacked was soon happen if the battle continued. I myself, and many others informed him that our involvement with North Vietnam was a huge mistake.

It was costing many of lives and even the religious Buddhist priests were setting themselves on fire and shit trying to put an end to the battle. Once the media got a hold of this the President knew that he had to put an end to this.

The President has always had back problems and had to take medicine, but now he was taking sleeping pills trying to get some sleep because he could not sleep knowing the slaughter that was going on from the bombing. I remember him once saying, children like my own are dying and they don't even know why? He then waited a little while and said, I don't know either?

As I looked at him with tears in his eyes and his head pointing partly down, as he lifted his hand to wipe the tears from his eyes. I knew then that he had made up his mind that he was going to put an end to the United States involvement in Vietnam.

Unfortunately, for him and this country that would not going to be an easy task. As we held meetings at the White House, staff and generals who got us involved was totally against us withdrawing from Vietnam.

After many meetings the President knew that he could never get the approval to end this war. He was even threatened that if he tried that Congress would go against him and even persuade the people of the United States that he was weak.

America picked a President who is too weak to fight for its allies or even country. They screamed that we cannot send a message to the world that we will allow the Communist backed regime win. I have never seen the hatred that I saw bestowed up on this President who only wanted to stop the vicious murdering of mostly innocent children.

No matter how much we tried to convince them that it was not working. For adding more troops would only turn a cold war into a boiling hot bloody war that will not end up with nothing but millions of poor lost lives. We would only be delaying the inevitable and no matter what we did all signs pointed to Vietnam becoming Communist.

The President stressed that we must put an end to what is going on. We need to start rebuilding a strong relationship with their government. We have other Communist countries that we can work with. Through time, I am sure that we will convince all of them to favor our type of democratic government over any form of government be it Communist or whatever.

We cannot enforce anyone to accept or deny any form of government. Are not America, who believe in the right to choose one's government, no matter if you are an American citizen or live in a foreign country. We all know that most of the people in Vietnam want a Communist government, be it right or be it wrong, it is not for us to make that decision for them.

People learn from their mistakes, as I am sure that they will and in time they will see where the grass is greener. They will see the light at the end of the tunnel, and with common sense they will eventually choose our way over the Communist way.

However, they must choose, not be forced, especially when it will cost us and them so many innocent lives. We must withdraw for the good of this country, for the good of their country and for the good of God, we cannot let this killing continue.

Yet, it seems that no matter what the President said, it was not going to change their decision. Of course, he could overrule them and present his case to the people in hope that they would side with him.

However, the timing was not right. An election was coming up and he knew that his opponent would surely be able to win over him if members of Congress and the military spoke out against him if he ended this Vietnam battle.

That is when we decided that the war started secretly and that it should end the same way. Publicly, his hands were tied for surely, he would lose the White House if he spoke out to end the battle.

His opponent would surely use this as weakness instead of kindness for innocent lives. He had no certainty that he would be elected, he knew if he did not, the next President would probably escalate the war as more lives are destroyed. Even his vice-president did not side with him wholly, because he felt that we would be seen as weak. What was he to do?

Our intelligence told us that for the right price that those who were near to the South Vietnam regime. Who with our help could take out the Diem government leaders and then we would be able to bring an end to this war before any more innocent civilians lives are taken.

The CIA sent in operatives and was quickly carried out the assassination and we were now on the path of bringing an end to the Vietnam battle, I thought, but I should have known better. The power that I call the Secret Society did not take long to see what the President had planned.

Let me just say that about three weeks later, I watched on my living room's tv as I saw our President assassinated before my eyes. I knew who had did it, but what could I do. The Vice President was sworn in almost immediately and the war was back in full force again.

So, what happens, the Gulf of Tonkin and from that lie of a false attack, finally they were able to get the new President to send in more troops that soon eventually led us into an all-out war.

The Gulf of Tonkin Resolution that gave the President the power to increase military presence and invading all the international borders. Like all wars, the President felt this war once we did a full attack would not last long. Boy, was he wrong.

As America found itself in a major war that the President was persuaded by his staff and generals would not even last a year. The war went on a whole lot longer than anyone expected. Just like with the previous President it took a big tow on the present one. As we could see him aging as more and more poor innocent lives were being wasted on Vietnam soil. When it came time for the President to run for re-election, he made it perfectly clear...I shall not seek, and I will not accept, the nomination of my party for another term as your President.

America has been tricked and forced into wars all throughout the history of this country. For some strange reason, it always seems to work. We can look back at the major wars. The World War I and World War II the same similar tricks were used for them to get the American people to get upset and end up going to war.

Lusitania sank on May 7, 1915. A year earlier, the war was started after the assassination of Archduke Ferdinand. The President wanted to go to war, but the U.S. people did not. He knew that only if the Germans was to attack the United States would the American people be willing to get into the war.

So, he decided that if we could not join the war openly, we could at least assist them. We loaded ammunition onto the Lusitania and used the cruise liner to transport weapons and arms to support the fight against Germany. However, eventually the German found out and they sent out their submarines and to teach us a lesson, they blew it up. The United States first reported that the German blew up the ship for no reason but to kill innocent passengers.

Yet, the Congress soon received information of what really happened. While the American people for some time always thought that the German torpedo the ship for no reason, killing innocent passengers.

They were ready to go to war, but Congress knew the real story. So, we did not join into the war until after a year later and it had nothing to do with the Lusitania.

Once again it was based on lies and greed. It was called the Zimmerman Telegram, like our recent Lies of WMDs. The intelligence is recorded of notifying the President about a telegram that they intercepted. Since, today we know the telegram never existed, it is a pretty sure bet, that it was really the President and staff who came up with it.

The President and many others, especially the rich who had investments in the countries that was involved in the war. If Germany continued to win, a lot of rich Americans who had money and property in those country was going to lose a lot. A lot of pressure were put on the President and members of Congress. Unfortunately, not enough of them to have the U.S. enter the war.

So, then the Zimmerman Telegram appeared, a coded message from Germany to Mexico. The message explain that Germany was going to get the Mexican to join on their side and for doing so they would give them a third of the United States. They needed for the Mexicans to allow them to go through Mexico, so they could get to the border of the United States.

Due to this fake Zimmerman Telegram, enough Congress member voted for the United States to enter the war. During this war, over ten million soldiers died and over 20 million were wounded. Also, many millions of civilian lives were sacrificed as well. The war that many thought would be the war to end all wars, did not as later World War II started.

The President and his military advisors were piling up weapons to attack Japan. The American people, after World War I had no desire to get into another war.

There were not enough members of Congress, who had the nerve to ask them to go through what they have went through in World War I.

The President had made up his mind to get into the war one way or the other. The only problem was how was he going to be able to do it with the approval of the Congress or the American people. The main reason for the President wanting to go to war because of the pressure from the rich who worried about their investments oversea.

The average American was against it, but the richest people in the country were the ones who determined that we got involved. It did not matter how many poor people lives were lost. To please the rich and to ensure them that we would get involved with World War II. We started setting up for it by loading up weapons and military equipment in Hawaii.

Hawaii was not far from Japan and we knew that we could quickly fly and sail over to attack them once we figured out a way to get the American people to let us. To please the rich, the President invoke a draft bill that every male 21-30 had to sign up.

For what they refer to as the Selective Training Act. This was to ensure that we would legally be able to draft all the people we needed for World War II.

While this was going on, we continued to build up more warfare over in Hawaii. The

Japanese were not stupid, they saw the buildup in Hawaii and they quickly notified the United States to remove it.

The President paid them no mind as we continued building it up. They then sent ambassadors over to the United States to make it perfectly clear that they would not sit idly by while we set up a brigade to attack them.

Several times, they threaten us and made it perfectly clear. If we did not remove the weapons and military from Hawaii, then they had no choice but to do it themselves. As all these threats were going on back and forth, all the while the war was going on and Hitler was winning country by country.

The Japanese finally attacked our naval base, Pearl Harbor, in Hawaii. The President knew that they were going to carry out their threats. What fool would just sit there and allow someone to build up their military right at their doorstep, while they sit quietly to be attacked.

Japan knew what the United States were doing and just like when you know a big bully is going to fight you, it always best to get your lick in first.

Was the United States military so stupid that they did not see this even coming? Even after the warning and threats from Japan? If the White House had notified the military at Pearl Harbor, they would have been ready for the attack.

With all the planes and ships, they should have been able to take out the Japanese air attack even before it reaches the Hawaii shores.

We knew that we had enough military to prevent the attack, so if we had them prepare for it, they would have successfully demolished the Japan's simple air attack and what then. The American would have said, we told you we had nothing to worry about. They tried us, and we whipped them, so we never have to worry about them attacking us again. We will remain out of the war, it is not our problem.

However, what if we make sure that the military is not notified and prepared for an attack. What if we jammed our own radar so they will not be able to launch ships and planes to attack before the Japanese reach Hawaii's shore.

Just enough so that Japan reaches the shore and that they attack our military base. We can claim that they did it out of the blue and we had no idea that they were going to do it.

We will lose some lives and some military equipment, but then we will have an excuse to finally get into this war and make the rich people happy. Of course, no one expected to lose so many lives. Yet, the key was to make the American people so upset that they would accept us going into war.

Now, that we were at war and due to the mandatory selective draft, we knew that we would have enough people to fight another world war and hopefully end it quickly without too many deaths. Most of all, save and secure the rich man's investments overseas.

World War II lived up to its name. When the war finally ended over sixty million lives, military and civilians, were lost. One can only wonder if there is another World War how many millions of lives will be lost then. Yet, as we continue to have wars, we know the question is not if it will happen, but when it will happen?

The American people have been lied to time and time again and every time they have fell for it. It is believed that Abraham Lincoln once said, you can fool some of the people all the time and all the people some of the time, but you cannot fool all the people all the time. I am not sure that applies to the American people?

All throughout history, time and time again the government have been able to lie and deceived the American people time and time again. Even when they find out that they have been fooled such as the lies of WMDs, the government is still able to carry out the mission. Without the American people demanding an end to the war once they found out that they had been tricked into it.

As long, as the American people continue to have a corrupt and dishonest political system, the same will continue to happen years and years from now.

A government can only be as good as the people who can run and be elected. Even when they are elected by a very small minority. When more than half of the people in the country are so fed up with politician's lies that they have an apathy not to vote.

Those who do vote usually end up with it almost split down the middle on who gets into office. So, a minority of less than a quarter of the people get to choose their leader. No wonder most of the people are unhappy about the way the country is being run.

Even today, most people do not understand how the Iran Nuclear Deal came about. Why now, why after so many years after the takeover of the Shah. After the fall of the Shah of Iran, who was one of our puppets that we were able to control. Once he was overthrown, we lost our internal connection with the country.

Of course, since he was our loyal puppet we had to allow him to come to the United States. The dumb reason that we gave was that we were not trying to protect him, but for medical reasons.

No one believed the nonsense that he was sick and only a United States physician could cure him. The people of Iran knew that he was our puppet and they were determined to behead him.

The people of Iran were furious that we saved him when they wanted him to get the punishment he deserved for the cruel way he treated the Iranian people.

Soon a group of Iranian students realized that the United States were in such a rush to save the Shah that they left their own Americans vulnerable at the Embassy.

Our own government that knew that shit had hit the fan. That the country was being taken over and they had no problem in securing a safe exit for the Shah, when weeks earlier they could have evacuated our embassy. That was not
their priority.

The Iranian student went to the Embassy and rounded up every single one of the diplomats and had them imprisoned. They used the diplomats as leverage to get the United States to return the Shah. They threaten to kill all the diplomats if the Shah was not returned.

The White House ignored their demands and by doing so risked the lives of all the

American diplomats for one crooked brutal Shah. Luckily, for the diplomats the people of Iran decided that it was not right to kill those who were just innocent pawns by their government.

They decided that they would not kill them mainly because they knew it would not bring the Shah back. So, they decided that they also could not release them and hopefully if they held them long enough the American people would demand their return and they would get the Shah. Of course, as you know as days went into weeks and weeks went into months, the American diplomats remained as Iran's hostages.

Many of the military hawks wanted the President to invade Iran to get the hostages. The President knew that by doing that it would not only cost the lives of all the hostages, but many more thousands of lives as well depending on how long the war lasted.

The President found himself in a catch 22, he could not return the Shah because the Shah was a close ally to the United States. If he did not protect him than others who were puppets of ours would feel that we would not protect them as well. While at the same time the American people were screaming for us to bring the American diplomats home.

The President knew how the Vietnam War that had just ended costed us over sixty thousand lives. A war against a country like Iran would cost us a whole lot more. He had no choice as some would say, other than to just wait and pray. That what he did as the hostages remain in Iran with no plan to get them out.

The President decided to try another plan instead of an all-out invasion. The

President invoked the Executive Order 12170 which froze over $12 billion dollars of Iran's money that had been deposited in overseas banks. The next move was for a sanction that would affect their economy and maybe the people of Iran would then demand their new government to release the hostages.

It was everything that could be done other than to release the Shah. Many felt that the plan would work but as time went on we were proven wrong. The people were very upset with Americans being hostages and by the President protecting our puppet, he lost re-election.

When the new President came in office, the Iranian decided to offer an olive leaf since the administration had changed. They called the new President and informed him that the hostages would be released. This made the new President look good and finally put an end to the long carried out ordeal.

Once all the hostages had been returned to the United States, the Iranian then expected us to return the favor. They expected for us to stop all the sanctions and allow them access to their money in the overseas banks. It did not happen.

Now, Iran felt like that they had been slapped in the face. After they released the hostages, the new President did not give them anything in return. That was not only a slap in their face, but it also was what motivated them to start a program to create Nuclear Weapons.

Now, back to our original question, why after over fifty years did the United States decide to lift sanctions and return the money. Money that now had accumulated to over $100 billion dollars.

What the American people was told for the reason for the Iran Nuclear Deal is totally different from the real reason. If we felt that we could trust a promise by them to not create Nuclear Weapons, surely, we could have done that many years ago.

For you see the truth of the matter was not that they made a promise not to create Nuclear Weapons, but that they promised not to use them. Since what went down after the returning of the hostages, the Iranians knew that the only way they would ever get their money back is through force. The kind of force of a Nuclear Bomb would be the only way to get their money back.

It took them some time before they were able to achieve Nuclear success. However, once our intelligence notified us that they had successfully accomplished that. We decided that after all these years, maybe it was time for us to have a little congenial sit down and chat.

It now was no longer worrying that they would get upset and take our strong military on against their weak military. Now it was Nuclear Bomb against Nuclear Bomb and in that type of war nobody wins.

Due to us not obliging them when they returned the hostages, where we could have just release their funds and called it even. Now years later we found ourselves face with someone who we certainly did not want to have as an enemy.

So, we did the only reasonable thing that we could possibly do. We finally returned them the money and got rid of the sanctions and decided that it would be best for us to be friends than enemies now that they had the BOMB.

# Chapter Five

There is so much that goes on in our government that the average citizen knows nothing about. Not only the citizens, but sometimes not even the President himself. As I remember the time that one of the General became a little famous when he asked the question., who's in charge? Believe me, I have heard that question more than once during all my years in service.

We are made up of so many different groups and subgroups that sometimes no one can keep track. If it is the individual levels of the FBI, CIA, Secret Service, or less transparent covet groups. It is very easy sometimes for one hand not to know what the other hand is doing.

One of the best examples of this was the alleged killing of Osama Bin Ladin. Osama Bin Ladin who was wrongfully accused of the 911 attack on this country. After intelligence (both nationally and internationally) proved that Saddam Hussein had nothing to do with it.

The people who were involved over ten years with the investigation of the 911 attack knew that Osama had nothing to do with it. He was just a quick decoy or scapegoat to cover up the real people responsible since the American people were starting to ask who did it, if not Hussein?

Everyone back then that needed to know, knew that Bin Ladin was not a problem. It was just our plan A that had fallen apart, and we then quickly came up with plan B that allowed us to invade Iraq to prevent any chance of the American people obtaining cheaper Iraq oil over Saudi's oil.

So as years went pass, no one heard a squeak from Bin Ladin and everything was going fine. The war was still going on and we had advanced, not only into Afghanistan, but Libya and some of Syria. There was an election coming up and we thought that the President would have his mind solely on campaigning and getting re-elected to the White House.

The race for the White House looked close and I for one thought that the President was fully concentrated on that. Not concerned about someone or something that took place years earlier before he took office. Especially, since as far as Bin Ladin, everything had been quiet and when things are quiet, I was always taught it is best not to stir things up, let it rest. Under the previous President's administration, it was decided that there would be some things that the new President did not need to know.

There were a few things that was decided on that there was no need to know as far as the President was concerned. Usually, this has been done in many new White House administration, it was nothing new. However, this time it back fired on us.

The previous admiration after using Bin Ladin as a scapegoat, a year or so later, we created a Bin Ladin Disclosure Agreement with Bin Ladin. It was when we accidentally found Bin Ladin while chasing down someone else.

This was pure luck, especially since we constantly feared that somehow, he would be able to convince the American people that he had nothing to do with 911. Then once again they would be asking, if not him then who?

There was a lot of evidence that he could use to prove that he had nothing to do with 911. Many were coveted spies who were working over in the Middle East. It pays to have friends in the right places. Not only did they possess the proof that Bin Ladin had nothing to do with 911, but also proof on who did?

When this was brought to the counsel attention. We did not want to risk the chance of the country finding out who was behind 911. Not only that, but some of us feared that if we killed Bin Ladin, he would become a martyr and possibly cause Middle East terrorists to attack our country.

After a couple of days of discussion, while he was being held over in the Middle East, we decided what would be best for us all including him would be a Truce. Where we would let him live and not imprison him, but that he could not have any contacts with anyone accept his family and a few close friends. As far as the world would know, he just vanished from the earth.

This is not the first time that we made a so-called Truce with an enemy. Only a few chosen ones were involved in our Truce with Adolf Hitler. Just like with Bin Ladin, we did not want a martyr or any sympathizers who would come about if we took him to court and executed him. Few knows about this closed Truce, but we also have had open Truces.

After we had our closed Truce with Hitler, his partner in crime, should we say, wanted the same Truce except he was not going to go into hiding. Since, we knew that he knew about our closed Truce with Hitler, we had no alternative available for us.  We gave Hirohito an open Truce.

Luckily, everyone was so glad that World War II was over, no one even questioned it. The American people were just glad that all the killings of millions of people were over.

They were too excited with the celebration that their love ones were finally coming home, that many just assumed that Hitler got blown up during the war.  We all know that only the unfortunate pawns die in war, while the leaders always have a quick escape plan.

So, after capturing Bin Ladin we decided to have a close Truce with him. We knew that there was no place in the United States where we could hide him.  Since he insisted on being in his homeland, we decided to put him as close as possible.  This is how Afghanistan's neigbor Pakistan came into play.

Many of us did not like the idea of him remaining close to home.  I felt that it would be better to put him out on an isolated island somewhere.  Just like Napoleon when he was captured, he was placed on an island to live out the rest of his life.  He survived quite well on the island of Saint Helena in the deep part of the Atlantic Ocean.

It was finally decided that Bin Ladin would be placed in a protected compound in Pakistan.  The Pakistani gov't was against it, but later the White House was able to persuade them.  Bin Ladin would be in a secured living quarters with guarded security and could not at any time leave the compound. His family who would be living with him would have access only to the local area and they would be monitored whenever they left the compound.

He would be a free man to a point, his love ones would be by his side and all he had to do was to disappear from society. Since Bin Ladin considered himself a peaceful man, who joined the battle against Russia who had invaded a fellow Muslim country. After successfully defeating Russia and having them to withdraw from Afghanistan, he felt that he had fulfill his purpose in life.

So, through agreement on both sides, we made a closed Truce with him that his life would be spared, and he would have no outside contact with the rest of the world. The Truce was sealed and only those who needed to know, knew about this arraignment. The less people the better.

Everything seem to be going fine and for several years everything went along fine. Many people including the new President saw Bin Ladin as a terrible man who had done terrible things all over the world. Others like myself saw him as a freedom fighter, a Nat Turner, or if he had the choice to be non-violent a Malcolm X or even a Martin Luther King.

He was not a Hitler, as many chose to call him, for he never attempted to take over anyone's country or invade a country for his own gain. He went to Afghanistan to help the people there, fight against an invader who was attacking their country.

So, we made the right decision, but we had no idea of the consequences that would come about years later. As, I said earlier the new President did not know about our arraignment with Osama Bin Ladin. Neither did we know that the new President had created a private covet team that had been seeking Bin Ladin out for years.

Too many cooks in the kitchen, too many idle hands to be watched, or the left hand not knowing what the right hand is doing. There are many different groups of high level intelligence and each is working on different assignments. In the intelligence field, there are always spies and even those who are willing to be a traitor for the right price.

There aren't any co-operations between these different groups and we can only hope that those who are in a specific group, that inside that group there is not a spy. The least people you have involved, the less likely there will be a leak or a mole.

In this incident, a group selected by the present President was working on a case that was already closed, but they did not know this. Due to hard investigation and the right amount of money, they finally got a lead on Bin Ladin whereabouts.

We later found out that an agent in Pakistan had gotten in touch with the President's team and for the right amount of money lead them right to him. We knew that the only way that anyone could have found Bin Ladin, it had to be from someone that was inside who knew about the secret operation.

The President sent his team in and we did not find out about it until it was released after the completion of the operation. The helicopters had landed and Bin Ladin was taken from the compound. He was flown to a waiting ship and was on his way to the United States. Where he was to be charged for 911 to please the American people's hunger for justice and revenge.

It would have been a great front-page story, if it was not for the Truce or for the fact that he had nothing to do with 911. Even when he told us, he wishes he could have been able to pull off something that fantastic. However, he would not had directed it at the innocent people in the twin towers. He would have had it directed at the White House, Congress, and the Pentagon only.

I will never forget that night, I can only imagine the look on Bin Ladin's face when the operation took place and he found out that it was us doing it. I could see him all bewildered and saying, but you promise, you promise, what about our Truce?

By the time the President let us in on his operation, it was too late to prevent it, but we knew we had to stop it. Luckily, Bin Ladin was not killed during the fire fight at the compound. They had killed some others who were protecting him, but Bin Ladin was verified and only kidnapped from his home.

Once we discovered what had went down, we had no choice but to now tell the President about the Truce and try to figure out a way out of this. Which was not going to be easy since the Presidential press core had been notified and did not hesitate to spread the news.

Was the President upset after we informed him? Upset could not describe the look on his face as we explain the Truce that took place several years ago. We explained that Bin Ladin could not be brought to the United States and had to be returned to Pakistan. We had to figure out a new hideout for him, hopefully this time somewhere out in the middle of the ocean.

Pakistan had gotten in touch with us and was raising hell. As one of the officials said, you have the patients running the asylum, nobody knows what the hell is going on? It was a mess and we knew that we had to quickly clean it up. The first thing we did was to notify the ship to come to a complete stop. We then had Pakistan to send out a ship to retrieve Bin Ladin.

Someone said, I can see tomorrow's news headline. U.S. captured the great terrorist Osama Bin Ladin, only to let him go. It is like catching a fish and then dropping it back into the water after spending all day fishing for it. Who is going to release to the press that somehow the fish slipped from our hands and got away?

We knew that we could not tell the American people about the Truce. For surely, it would not set well. We also explained to the President that we could not kill Bin Ladin. He and his associates had valid provable information that Saudi Arabia was involved in 911. If that information came out, then the Saudis would immediately throw us under the bus and the whole world would find out that we were the ones who attacked our own country.

The President had no choice but to send Bin Ladin back. However, the big question now was what were we going to tell the American people? No one had a clue; the news media had been notified that we had pulled off the operation and had Bin Ladin on a ship on his way to the U.S. shores.

That when we came up with something that many of us felt did not make any sense. Since we knew that we had to return him back to Pakistan and that the people were expecting him. Someone first came up with just say that he died on the way and we can just wrap up something that look like a body and carry it off the ship because we knew the press would be there.

However, we also knew that if we said we had a dead body that the media and especially conspiracy theorist would not be satisfied with a dummy corpse. They would demand DNA and whatever to verify 100% that it was Osama Bin Ladin.

We were back at point one and since we knew we had to return Bin Ladin, the only thing someone came up with is to say that he was killed at the compound and we decided to give him a naval burial at sea.

Someone quickly spoke up, what the hell, he was never in the military, let alone in the navy? I don't think Muslim believe in water burials, they want land burials or cremation. You are going to tell the American people
that you risked troops lives, after killing Bin Ladin. Having them carry his dead body, not only to a helicopter and then have it place on a ship that is on its way to our shores, and then decided, what the Hell, let us just dump his ass in the water. We don't need to verify to any one that it is him, they will just take our word for it.

This does not make any damn sense? If he was dead and you did not want the body to be brought back to prove that he was dead? While go through risking your troop lives dragging his body onto the helicopter and then placing it on a ship?

Another Senator spoke up, "Also, this is not the first time that there were claims that he was dead, trust but verify, we have

140

to prove that it is him.  So, why after having his dead body would we dump it in the ocean instead of bringing it back, so the body can be officially proven to be his.  So, the world will know that we got him!"

"Especially", said another agent, "after the lies of WMDs do you think anyone would believe that shit?"  "The Republican candidate will be the first one to say it was a hoax from the very beginning, to raise the serving President up in the polls".  "This shit will never work, it totally does not make any sense?"

Then someone else said, "Well if you can come up with a better idea, we all would like to hear it?"  "The media has already been notified that we got Bin Ladin, the President's writers are creating a speech as we speak."  "We know that we are not going to tell the American people about the Truce, so what the hell do you have to put on the table?"

After about ten seconds of silent, he then said, "I thought so."  "No matter how ridiculous it may sound, we don't have time to try to come up with something better."  Inform the President that this is our story for him to give to the American people and no matter how dumb it sounds, we are sticking to it.

"Yes", said one of the Senators, all we must do is tell the media not to ask any questions about why we dump him in the sea, uh just like we with WMDs, the media will help us pull this off?"  "Cause those rich bastards got more to lose than us."

"Just like the media did with the lies of WMDs, we control them, or I should say they do."  Another Senator, shouted out,

"Shut up, you need to put down that cannister you keep in your coat pocket, before you end up in a fatal accident down the road!"

Reluctantly, while Bin Ladin was returned, we told the American people that was the way it went down. We figured that the conspiracy theorist would have a field day with it, but we had no better explanation to present. I was shocked that the American people accepted it and the President won re-election.

I remember talking to some of my colleagues who also was surprised that the American people fell for it. I remember one of them saying, my friend you do not know the American people? They will believe anything they see on the news, if it is in color. A few of the guys laughed as one said, "You are right, they fell for the Weapons of Mass Destruction after seeing it, repeatedly, on the news.

Another one said, yeah but it does not even have to be in color for them to fall for it. Remember the moon landing was in black and white. One of the younger guys spoke up, the moon landing? Yeah kid, the older guy said, it may had been before your time, but you know that we said we landed on the moon once, right?

"What." said the young guy, "we did land on the moon, like way back in the 60's."
Some of us older guys busted out laughing. "Hey kid", said the older guy, "have you ever seen the surface of the moon?" "Yeah, said the young guy, I saw it on tv." "I didn't see it live, but we have film documentary of the landing and the walking on the moon."

The older man joked saying, "Have you ever seen Superman on tv?" "Do you think that he can really fly?"  We all laughed as the older man said, "Kid if we went to the moon before you were born, fifty years ago, why is it that we never went back?"  "All this time we should have high rise apartments up there by now."

We all laughed as the young man looked stunned?  The older man said, "With all your young people fancy computers, don't you think our rocket technology has improved since the 1960's."  "If we went there back then, don't you think we would have an airport up there by now."

Then another guy pointed his finger toward a window and said, "Hey look kid, it's a bird, no, it's a plane, oh no it's Superman."  We all laughed and got up and left as the kid just sit there stunned probably wondering why, if we went to the moon fifty years ago, why is it that we never went back to the moon?

It is true today, just as much as it has been in the past, that people will believe whatever they want to believe.  We are taught early in life how to believe in lies, as early as adolescent.  We are told early in life that the stork brought us.  That a fat man in a red suit brings us toys, or a big bunny delivers us eggs.  A little fairy put money under our pillow when we lose a tooth.

Anyone can see why we are so gullible to believe in lies.  We are taught at an early age.  Who was it, P.T. Barnum who said something like there is a sucker born every minute.

How can a married woman not know that her husband is cheating on her when everyone else in the neighborhood knows?  Simple, because people only believe what they want to believe, no matter what the evidence and truth says.

Remember Wiki-leaks, due to Wiki-leaks, receiving information about a trail of money coming from Saudi Arabia. The Saudi's hijackers who were on the plane that was involved in 911, proof came out that also that Saudi Arabia financed it to some degree.

Due to the leak reaching the American people, the Congress felt that they had no choice than to at least allow the families of the victims to sue the Saudi Arabians for their involvement.

Yet, the White House and others who felt that this could open-up a can of worms. If the Saudis are pressured, they may then leak who else was involved and that would not be a good thing for the former White House.

Everyone knows, for some outsider to pull off something that big, they would have to had inside help. Hopefully, someday enough American people will want to know the truth and demand a 911 investigation! Yet, enough evidence has already been available to credit an investigation, so I will not hold my breath.

The lawsuit is not anyone's worry. If Saudi Arabia was found responsible for any lawsuits, we all know that they would not need to pay. The United States government would pay any lawsuits and just say that Saudi Arabia did. They would have no choice for fear that the Saudis would leak out that we were the main culprit due to greed and money.

The White House does not want to upset the Saudis. They know if the American people found out that their own government was involved in the 911 attack, it would not matter if the Saudis or any other country participated.

The country would only blame the crooked government that we have, since they would see that the Saudis benefitted, but it could had not been carried out without our government involvement.

One may say that it is terrible that a government would do something as horrendous as 911 upon its own people just because of greed and money. Yet, with the lies of WMDs which was for the same reason, many more have died than those who died during 911. 911 was set up to benefit the Saudis, the American oil companies, and the rich investments over in Saudi Arabia.

With the war that was based upon lies of WMDs, it has not only cause more death, but also a greater amount of money for the insiders who benefits from it especially American contractors.

I am convinced that the American people do not want to know the truth because they cannot handle the truth. So, they just ignore it and close their eyes and hope that it does not get any worse. Like a person who feel sick and feel the huge lump in their breast but ignores it because they do not want to face the consequences.

It is not due to 911 that I am writing this. For it seems that the American people do not care, so why should I. No, the reason that I have chosen to finally speak out now is not because of 911. Not for the lies of WMDs, but because of something much worse. The reason that I speak out now is because I have recently found out who the Secret Society is.

If it was not for a Senator, who had been very close to me for many years. I would have never been able to discover who the real people were that we only refer to as the Secret Society. I also would not have found the strength to finally release these documents. If it had not been what he told me while I was talking to him on his death bed.

For many years, I knew that there was this Secret Society that practically ran the entire country, as far as politicians and rich capitalists were concerned. Many others have spoken about them and how they control the basic American dollar in our country. They have control of the banking and financial institution systems.

As well in the last twenty years, it has taken over our national media. The best example of this was the lies of WMDs. Unlike the Watergate Scandal, where an open and honest media that was for the public interest, instead of controlled by a monopolized mind control media.

A lot of good honest caring reporters wanted to investigate both 911 and the WMDs. However, the few owners of the large stations made sure that assignment was not given out.

During Vietnam, it was the American people who finally put an end to the war. Due to the honesty, righteousness and the courage of the media to see to it they delivered the truth to the American people. Unlike what we have today, the media had honor and were respected and trusted by the American people.

The White House and Congress tried to hide the Vietnam war from the American people. However, the media back then felt an

obligation to the American people and felt that they should know the truth. The media felt that the people had a right to know and was not about to have a government overrule the truth that the
people seek.

Back then, the media disregarded the demands placed upon them by the government, as they chose to put the people first. When they had reporters at the bases showing planes flying in and unloading body bags of Americans. They sent their reporting staff right onto the battle-field so America could get a real live look at what was happening.

Due to the media, the war was no longer a distance thing, but was brought right to the American people's doorstep. They made America realize that war was no game. That war takes lives, that war is hell, and this is where your fellow Americans are dying, while you sit comfortably at home.

When the camera scan over the mass of dead bodies and bloody parts that seem to be scattered everywhere. The American people looked at their tv sets in their living rooms and they saw more than they could even imagine. As they saw not only dead soldiers, but innocent bodies of women and children. They saw blown up bodies of civilians and were able to hear the agony cries of their pain and suffering.

It was only then, thanks to the media, the American people realized that war was not a game of toy soldiers. No, for the American people saw with their own eyes, that war was nothing more than a mass destruction of lives. The blown off legs, the severed heads and bloody torsos.

The poor refugees, mostly children starving with that simple look on their face that simply ask... why?  This is what ended the Vietnam War, the Media!

Many know that we lived in a country where the rich always seem to get richer, while the poorer get poor.  They know that the top of the top of one percent seem to have all the money.  Yet, it was not until the downfall of the economy around 2008 that made many realize the disaster that comes when you allow a small group to control the financial structure.

A downfall or a recession, whatever you may choose to call it, does not occur over night.  Since the Great Depression in the late 1920s our government set up a system to prevent what occurred in 2008.

However, in 1999 the White House and many members of the Republican party got rid of the Glass-Steagall Act.  The Glass Steagall Act was a banking act of 1933 that limited commercial banks and securities firms.

This open a floodgate for scams and criminal activities.  Many banks were now able to loan money out to businesses and private individuals.  Which they knew did not have the capability to repay the loans.  It was a simple win-win for the banks.  They would loan money, accept the down payment, and receive a low monthly payment until the loan ballooned, when they would then foreclose on the property.

It worked well as greed continued to grow as the cost of houses went higher and higher.  Everyone knew that eventually the housing market would burst.

However, the bank knew that they had nothing to worry about because the fix was already in for the government to save or bail them out.

By raising the house price sky high, that made sure that most people would not have the twenty percent to put down. So, working with crooked insurance companies and house appraisers they just charged the mortgage insurance to the note. This way the bank would be compensated.

The Private Mortgage Insurance protected the bank, not the purchaser of the house. So, no matter how jacked up the price on the house was set up to, the bank could not lose. Once again, the richer would get richer and the poor buyer would get poorer.

Also, while the Glass-Steagall Act was gone, Wall Street wanted in on the corrupt action as well. So, with the use of hedge funds and falsifying stock rates with no government control, they had a field day. The American investors were set up for the biggest stock scam ever. They already had pre-approval from the White House that they would be covered. Isn't America great?

We all knew that there were key people who really ran the country, not just one person who we call President. Most of us assume it was just some old rich people like Rockefellers, Carnegie, Dupont, etc., like it was in the old days. Unfortunately, that night I found out that it was much worse than just some rich people.

As I sat with my close friend on his death bed, we discuss all the little things that one enjoys during life. We did not talk about our work or the awful things that we had done. We talked about our families, our love ones, our grandchildren, even how each of us first fell in love.

The joy of having a close friend and how friends should never keep secrets from each other. That when he said, my old friend, there is one secret that I have kept from you.

I remember how I reacted when he said that. The look that came across his face and the look in his eyes. A quick thought came to my mind that I hope he is not going to tell me that he has been having an affair with my wife? He then started speaking as he said, you know the Secret Society that you are always talking about. I know who they are, and they do control our country.

He told me how he found out a few years ago. Once they felt that he was trustworthy enough not to expose them to the American people. He then proceeded to tell me that he was at the White House during a dinner party with some foreign leaders. He was later pulled aside and met with the Vice President and some others in a private room.

During that meeting, he was told that he had earn the honor to meet the Secret Society. After some more discussion, they then went back to the dinner. Later after the dinner party ended, he had a blindfold placed over his eyes.

He recalled how he felt like a new freshman at a college initiation. Only he did not know if they were going to take him to see the Secret Society or if they were taking him somewhere to be shot. Luckily for him it was not the latter.

He remembered being lead to an elevator and travelled downward for what seemed like forever.  He then walked for a while before he heard a door open.

He heard a lot of noise like people were celebrating a birthday party, or something like a rally.  He then was told that he could remove the blindfold.  He quickly raised it up from covering his eyes as he saw a whole lot of people.

People were chanting and cheering everywhere as he looked in the direction that they were looking.  That when he saw it!  A stage with a podium and the large background that was behind the stage. There behind the podium was a giant size swastika with the word HEIL FUROR!

That when my friend quickly realized that after all the millions of lives sacrificed during WWII, the Nazi party had not been demised.  They had been steadily rebuilding and planning for WWIII, only this time with the United States on their side. The best part of it all is that the American people would not even know that their country was under Nazi rule.

Therefore, we invaded the Middle East to make sure that we would have the Iraq oil available for us during the upcoming war.  As they continue to take over the Middle East and put in military bases everywhere. Preparing for once again for total world domination.

He then looked up at me sadly as he said, I am sorry that I had to tell you.  I just could not die without confessing it to someone, someone I know will be able to stop it.  As I looked at him, I did not know what to say, as I just slowly got up and left.

Asking myself, what was I going to do now, knowing what was about to go down.

Should I too remain silent as he has done knowing that it will take many years before they would be ready to take over the world. I would probably be dead long before they get to the point of taking over enough countries by coups and lies of WMDs, lies of chemical weapons, or attacks by us on our country and blaming it on the next country that they need to dismantle.

The documents ended there, as Jake Peterson did not know if he should believe what he had just read or not? He surely did not want to believe it, he like most Americans did not want to believe that his own government would do something like this.

Then he realized that it was not his government, not the government of the American people. It was now a government that was created by the American people, but now had been taken over by the Nazi Party!

For some reason, of all the three hundred million people in this entire country, it had ended up in his hands. He sits there just staring at the document that laid before him. He ponders at what his next move could be. He decided that something this big should not be given to his local newspaper, but to a bigger media like CNN or MSNBC.

Jake decided that he would get up early and deliver the documents to the head editor and that they would know the proper thing to do with it. He knew the American people had to know what it government was doing and how it had allowed Nazi corruption and evil to take over our Godly democracy.

Only the big media would have the connections to verify everything and convince the people to believe it so that it could be stopped.   However, since it seems that they are being controlled, he wonders if it would best to go to a small press to have them spread the news.

Jake gathered up all the papers and placed everything back into the briefcase. He was so excited that he started breathing hard as he took the briefcase into his bedroom.  He looked around his bedroom as his eyes searched for a safe place to put the briefcase.   He then decided that he would place it under the bed and push it back toward the wall.

He then undressed and started to get ready to go to bed.   He was so excited that he could not sleep.  He decided to watch some tv to help him calm down.   He started watching his television set and after a few hours, he finally became tired and fell asleep.

This is when he started to dream, to dream another awesome nightmare.   This time again he was going down a dark street as he suddenly heard someone behind him.  Just like before he felt a sharp object against his throat.  As he gasped for air and reached for his throat, he could see a face looking down at him.

As his eyes started to come more into focus, he could feel the warm blood running down his chest.  He quickly realized that this time he was not dreaming, for this was for real.    As he found himself taking his last breath as he gurgled as the blood flowed from his neck.  His focus became blurred as he started to lose consciousness.

The End

Lightning Source UK Ltd.
Milton Keynes UK
UKHW021855140421
381994UK00009B/111